The Hidden Life
of Polish Prisons

The Hidden Life
of Polish Prisons

Paweł Moczydłowski

INDIANA UNIVERSITY PRESS
Bloomington and Indianapolis

The paper used in this publication meets the minimum requirements of American
National Standard for Information Sciences—Permanence of Paper for Printed
Library Materials, ANSI Z39.48-1984.

Manufactured in the United States of America

Library of Congress Cataloging-in-Publication Data

Moczydłowski, Paweł, date
    The hidden life of Polish prisons / Paweł Moczydłowski.
        p.   cm.
    Translated from Polish.
    Includes index.
    ISBN 0-253-33861-1
    1. Prisons—Poland—Case studies. 2. Interpersonal relations—
Case studies. 3. Criminals—Rehabilitation—Poland—Case studies.
I. Title.
HV9715.7.M63 1992
365'.9438—dc20   91-47660

            1   2   3   4   5   96   95   94   93   92

Reality is endurable because it is not experienced as a whole. Nor is it experienced simultaneously. It reaches us in fractions of events, in shreds of realizations. Only reflection about it attempts to bring it together, immobilize it and understand it.

—Zofia Natkowska

Contents

Foreword

I met Paweł Moczydłowski at the Fourth International Conference on Penal Abolition late in May 1989 in Poland. Toward the end of the conference he brought me a manuscript. It was, he explained, an English translation of a sociological study of Polish prisons, which he had managed to publish in Poland in Polish under martial law. The Polish edition had rapidly gone out of print, and Polish authorities took a somewhat subtle approach to censorship: by allowing only a few hundred copies to be printed, the Polish authorities had soon been able to declare the book out of print. Paweł held out no hope of further publication in Poland. At his request, I smuggled his manuscript out of the country just two days before Solidarity triumphed and the Communist order rapidly collapsed.

I learned only this summer on a return visit to Poland the professional price Paweł and his Warsaw colleague Andrzej Rzeplinski paid for the original publication of Paweł's study. In 1982, they were banned from further prison visits. That ban was lifted only when Paweł himself became Director General of Polish prisons in April 1990. Andrzej is now one of the most active members of the Helsinki Human Rights Watch Committee and thus has access to any prisoner in Poland on demand. Paweł, Andrzej, and other Polish prison specialists work as a team to ferret out violations of prisoners' rights and redress them. The reforms they are undertaking together are among the more astonishing features of the political transformation of Poland.

Knowledgeable readers from outside Poland will readily see that the pre-reform prisons Paweł describes here have much in common with prisons the world over. The one major difference is that before 1989, Polish authorities required able-bodied male prisoners to work or suffer severe punishment. As a result, prisoner idleness was much less of a problem there than, for instance, in the United States. Prisoners were pushed hard not only in formal production but in hidden private production for the benefit of staff at all levels. What sets Paweł's study apart is that it does not describe prisoners alone or staff alone but relates with candor how staff and prisoners corrupt one another. I can only imagine how threatened authorities felt by the original publication of this work. Heavily engaged as they were in trying to stamp out the Solidarity Movement, they hardly needed these revelations to heighten public scorn for the regime. This book, like the massive circulation of underground literature under martial law, reflects the popular premise in Poland that their government is an alien force of self-serving crooks. This premise has made it acceptable for Polish scholars to be openly political and critical in their writing and to focus on the interaction of authorities and subjects far more freely than we are accustomed to seeing in Western literature. Paweł gets down to details of particular instances of horrific violence and human exploitation not as a fringe radical, but as a responsible mainstream social scientist. In so doing, his book contributes an extraordinarily authoritative, full and scathing account of prison life to the international literature.

Paweł writes that the Polish prison population exceeds 100,000, in a country that now has 40 million people in all. Recent Polish experience indicates an irony of dramatic political transformation—that many of the changes occur before the formal transformation. In 1986 the prison population reached 116,000. By the end of 1989, before Paweł assumed office, the population had dropped to 40,000. Only a few hundred of those released—in a final amnesty in 1986—were political prisoners. In addition, Polish Communist authorities repealed a Draconian provisional law, and, encouraged among others by the ombudsman's office they created in 1987, they continued to reduce the prison population dramatically by stages, culminating in the latest in a long series of amnesties in the fall of 1989. Also in 1989, the legal minimum cell space allocated to each prisoner was increased from a cubic meter minimum (easier to maintain in older prisons with higher ceilings) to a minimum of three square meters. The prison population has actually increased since Paweł assumed the directorship, reaching 58,000 or so last summer in adult prisons, with perhaps nine thousand more in juvenile institutions. Still, prison sentences have continued to decline and parole has been accelerated.

For their part, the new prison leadership of Paweł and his associate director, celebrated human rights lawyer Danuta Gajdus, has focused reform on staff-prisoner relations. In part, their initiative has been Draconian. Paweł is rather proud of reporting that 30 percent of the prison staff he started with has left the service—many through more or less voluntary retirement, and many by being fired. Paweł fires miscreants readily, swiftly, and almost routinely, and the Justice Minister always backs him up. A variety of people, including a prison director, ombudsmen, human rights watch visitors, and prisoners report that Paweł and Danuta have managed to convey that prisoner complaints will be taken seriously and that staff are as subject to regulations as the prisoners.

The sheer decline in prison overcrowding is given much credit for a change in the atmosphere in prisons, but I think equally important is a lesson Paweł has applied from this study of his. The more open a prison— the more prisoners have a chance to get out into the community (as in prison C in this book)—the less corrupt and violent are staff/prisoner relations. By law, prisoners who have served 30 percent of their sentence are eligible for weekly twenty-four-hour furloughs. And by Paweł's initiative, those who are eligible for furlough are likely to receive it. Now anyone in prison can have tea, while most of those who want vodka have merely to wait for a weekend opportunity to obtain it without guards' complicity, and need only sober up a bit before checking back into prison to avoid losing their privileges. Paweł even jokes that the tension in prisons is relieved by escape having become easier, telling me that facilitating escape is his major penal abolition initiative. The promise of furloughs is, I infer, the major factor in releasing the staff's grip on prisoners' daily existence on the one hand, and in giving prisoners an incentive to remain peaceful and obedient to regulations on the other.

Meanwhile, since 1989, work has become scarce, and so rather than being forced to work, prisoners compete to become "good" enough to earn wages. The guards no longer beat prisoners for being idle; instead they are more inclined to sympathize with the plight of idle prisoners.

I seriously doubt that corruption has been eliminated or that violence has disappeared. As my wife, fourteen-year-old daughter, and I freely toured Polish prisons this summer, I was struck by how highly disciplined prisoners are. Outside of solitary confinement, beds are meticulously made and cells are kept spotlessly clean and neat. Prisoners still stand at attention as one enters, in men's prisons at least, with an elder speaking first. I am convinced that prisoners are treated with considerably greater dignity and less abuse than before. I am convinced that prisons are considerably more peaceful and orderly than before. I am also aware that the prisoners are passive subjects of control, that they are still considered incompetent to shape their own regime, and that prison staffs have no more confidence in the prisoners' ability to succeed after release without recidivating than in the accounts Paweł offers here.

Sadly, prisoners continue to mutilate themselves in large numbers, and their strikes continue—some of them, such as refusing breakfast, pathetically ineffectual. This is especially true among recidivists facing long sentences, whose prospects of furlough or employment are remote, who, for instance, may see a best hope of relief in being removed to a hospital for treatment of a life-endangering condition. Paweł and others including legislative reformers such as Irena Rzeplinska recognize this problem and hope to shorten prison sentences still further.

As I left Poland last summer, it was rumored that Paweł might be asked to clean up the police for the Interior Ministry as he had succeeded at cleaning up the prison service for the Justice Ministry. For all the limitations inherent in sudden political reform, Paweł's is still a remarkable story of a scholar who has had the opportunity to apply academic lessons to real-world problems.

Hal Pepinsky
Bloomington, Indiana
November 14, 1991

Preface

In the 1970s and early 1980s Polish prisons rapidly filled up as the state pursued a strict penal policy in a situation of growing social discontent. The number of inmates and persons held in custody reached some 100,000. By the end of this period, every eighth adult male in Poland had experienced imprisonment. Not surprisingly, doubts emerged concerning the meaning and efficacy of the application of incarceration.

Such large-scale imprisonment accentuated the role of prisons as agents for resocializing their inmates, but no special successes in this area were noted. Official statistics showed that over 30 percent of Polish ex-convicts returned to prison. And everyday life experiences showed that most of them left the penitentiary worse people than they had been upon admittance—the prison demoralized. This divergence between the prisons' declared aims and the reality inclines one to seek causes, and it was my intention in this study to discover which features of these prisons made it impossible to realize the purposes of the penal system.

In the original Polish-language version of this study I discuss the psychosocial situation in prisons and its institutional conditioning. The manuscript has more than four hundred pages and includes numerous references to and presentations of the results of research conducted in the West (mainly in the United States). For Western readers such information is not new, and consequently I have limited the present book so that it contains only findings pertaining to Polish prisons, together with a number of references to Western studies.

The investigations which I carried out in Polish penitentiaries and the subsequent presentations of the collected material took several years of concentrated effort. The difficulties encountered in carrying out the research, putting the material into order, and editing it often inclined me to forsake my planned undertaking. That I was able to finish it is an achievement of many persons who, on the basis of my verbal reports or typed excerpts of the written work, convinced me that the effort was worth completing. I would like to express my gratitude to Professor Jacek Kurczewski and Professor Hanna Swida-Ziemba for discussing my work and offering comments in the course of its writing, to the workers of the Institute of Social Prevention and Resocialization at Warsaw University, and to the students of the Interdepartmental Penitentiary Group for their assistance and encouragement in continuing my task. Finally, I would like to thank the prison staff members and the prisoners themselves who made this book possible.

Warsaw, 1990

Introduction

The purpose of this study is to recreate an area of social reality that is often described as the "hidden life" of a prison—some investigators call it the "informal organization"—and to confront this reality with what heretofore were only theses about the sociology of the penitentiary.

The investigations in which I gathered material were not conducted in any conventional way. On many occasions I had opportunities to make close contact with prison reality and realized that my research could not be carried out using standard sociological techniques. I was compelled to work out my own methods to obtain data and to draw conclusions therefrom. As a result, I was faced with the necessity first of all of explaining the specific feature embedded in the prison organization that made it impossible to examine in a standard manner and then to show how this task could be effectively performed.

The first part of this book characterizes the nature of the protective wall that surrounds prisons and describes my methods of examination. This part, especially chapters 1, 2, and 3, is based on prison visits that I made before actually commencing my research. These experiences were gained at ten penal institutions (three for women, two for juvenile offenders, two for first offenders, three for recidivists) and at three boys' reformatories—all of which I stayed in during the 1970s and early 1980s.[1]

My actual research, the course of which was dictated by my earlier experiences, is described in chapter 4. It was conducted in three prisons: a closed penal institution for juveniles (institution A), a closed penal institution for recidivists (institution B), and a semi-open institution for first offenders (institution C).

The hidden life of a prison is generated by three groups of relations: those among prisoners, those among prison staff members, and those between prisoners and staff. The second part of this book describes all these groups of relations on the basis of my investigations at the three penitentiaries. Thus chapter 6 contains a description of relations prevalent among the prisoners in the three types of institutions and presents some ideas about the origins and functions of the informal structure of the prisoners' community. In chapter 7 I portray relations between the prisons staffs and the prisoners in the same three institutions. I also analyze these relations within the context of a formulated concept of relations among inmates. Similarly, chapter 8 provides a description of personal relations within the staff community. Chapter 9, finally, highlights my basic thesis, that the differentiation of social relations in the hidden life of Polish prisons is a derivative of their economic organization.

PART ONE

Thou Shalt Not Do Much Research

1.
A Reserved Terrain

The Informational Void

As most writers on the subject point out, it is the essential nature of penal institutions that the people placed inside them have limited contact with the outside world. Rarely is attention drawn to the two-sided nature of this isolation. Confinement, after all, constitutes a barrier that is impenetrable from both sides: the persons incarcerated cannot easily get out, and outsiders cannot easily get in. This fact, though quite obvious, seldom finds its way into our awareness, perhaps because of our aversion to the very image of being confined. But for scholars who would like to make their way inside and conduct research while retaining their outside identity, the barrier created by confinement is an essential fact.

The problem, as we shall see, is complex. It does not consist merely in overcoming confinement understood literally: closed doors, high walls, steep banks, and so forth. Entrance into this area of social reality that is closed to most of us poses a puzzle which I would like to solve in this part of the book. The task calls for understanding the peculiar nature of this barrier of confinement, which serves as much to protect the institution against probing by outsiders as it does to protect outsiders from the inmates.

The penal institution as a management system bases its inner organization on intervention in all domains of human life and strict scrutiny from above.[1] At the same time the prison is excluded from social oversight and remains at the complete disposal of political authorities. Political control is realized on one hand by the acceptance of hierarchic subordination as a style of management. The administrative-legal nature of relations creates for higher-level penal authorities an opportunity to wield an unlimited influence over the organization and functioning of those on a lower level. This relationship is often a dual dependence, personal (filling posts, giving promotions, handing out rewards and punishments) and official (the possibility of issuing unlimited directives). Chiefs at a certain level concentrate their attention on the requirements and expectations of persons or groups perceived as the source of their power. In turn the realization of those requirements and expectations becomes, on a similar principle, the object of the efforts of the subordinates.

On the other hand, being at the disposal of political authorities requires that members of the penal institution dissociate themselves from all possible involvement with events and movements in the society at large, which can be particularly dangerous for authorities during political crises.[2] The absence of these social influences results in a constant feeling of isolation on the part of members of the institution. Political authorities attain this effect above all by prohibiting any public airing of problems connected with the work of the prison staff. These functionaries are bound to regard as official secrets anything connected with their professional work.[3] Administrators of the institutions are also obliged to observe total silence about professional matters.

The void left by this absence of authentic articulation of problems is filled by propaganda versions—quite easily sniffed out by the public society. The lack of authentic information also leads to the spreading of information by persons who have had firsthand dealings with the institutions, and as a rule these are negative experiences.[4] Consequently, the public sees the staffs of these institutions as remaining outside its influence and thus possibly available to be used against it. The staffs, on the other hand, do not expect any positive support or acceptance from the public. This situation dooms the prison staffs to remain loyal to the authorities and to continue to suffer from a lack of communication with society. Furthermore, the authorities always have the means to control information about the institutions, even pejorative information, so as to keep a desired distance between the staffs and society. And the isolation is to a certain degree institutionalized, for staff members live together in separate buildings, relax in their own recreation centers, organize their own economic production in prison farms and factories, and so on.

The "Sacred Area"

Penal institutions serve above all to realize the political functions of a given social system. They are a negative aspect of the political system of a state that punishes those who break the law by limiting their freedom.

The prison thus fulfills a mission that is characteristic of political organizations: it influences other groups in order to force them to submit to its control.[5]

It is true that the prison system may also be viewed as an element of the *didactic* system of the state. But attempts at integrating the political and didactic functions have been, so far, mere illusory endeavors; the political functions dominate decisively. Even if the openly proclaimed intention of the penitentiary system is the resocialization of offenders, the function is still political.[6] The penitentiary system is closed to influence exerted by organizations that realize adaptive or educational functions—that is, those that prepare people for the roles imposed upon adult members of society—and it remains open to the impact of the political system.[7]

An apt illustration of this state of affairs in Poland is the extremely brief history (barely sixteen months long) of two associations, *Stowarzyszenie Pomocy Osobom Uwiezionym i ich Rodzinom,* or *Patronat* (the Association for Aid to Prisoners and Their Families), and *Polskie Stowarzyszenie Penitencjarne* (the Polish Penitentiary Association), whose aim was to assist people deprived of their freedom. *Patronat* attracted many well-known authors, artists, and scientists. The Polish Penitentiary Association emerged in an academic environment, attracting students, lawyers, criminologists, psychologists, sociologists, and teachers as well as persons professionally connected with the Department of Justice or centers cooperating with it, including judges, lawyers, curators, journalists, and publicists. After the proclamation of martial law on December 13, 1981, both societies were suspended. The fundamental controversial point was the government's demand that members of these groups refrain from visiting the penal institutions.[8]

The resistance of a prison system to contacts with academic centers has been explained by Robert Merton, who noted that

> science which asks questions of facts concerning every phase of nature and society comes into psychological, not logical, conflict with other attitudes toward these same data which have been crystallized and frequently ritualized by other institutions. Most institutions demand unqualified faith; but the institutions of science make skepticism a virtue. Every institution involves, in this sense, a "sacred area" which is resistant to "profane" examination in terms of scientific observation and logic.[9]

To the academic investigator in Poland, the most serious obstacle to research in prison has been not the conflict which "appears whenever science extends its research to new fields''[10] but the anticipation that such a conflict will be inaugurated by the prison system. A permanent consequence of this anticipation is the development by the penitentiary system of its own research activity, due to the absence of independent academic research in prisons.[11] Department of Justice centers have been set up whose employees are prison functionaries. Probably the intention was to ensure an attitude of loyalty, attachment, and respect on the part of the researchers.[12] These centers as well as the functionaries themselves concentrate on topics defined by the needs of the institution, reserving for themselves exclusive rights to research concerning the domains of social life controlled by the department.[13] Thanks to such narrow specialization, they regard themselves, within the subject range delineated by their bureaus, as more competent than, for instance, academic social scientists. The academic scholar therefore confronts a ''monopolist'' in trying to get access to data about a social field that remains under the latter's administration, a monopolist who also controls the state of knowledge on this particular subject.[14] In practice, studies pertaining to the prison system have to be approved for print by the central prison authorities, then passed by the state censorship office. The monopolist even claims the right to decide the veracity of statements made about prisons by other investigators.

Although academic scholars are permitted to conduct narrowly constricted research in penitentiaries, the problems which may become the subject of their studies are manipulated. Agreement to conduct investigations in prison calls for acceptance by the prison authorities of both the topic and the instruments which are to be employed in the investigations. Rejection of a proposed theme can be justified by stating that an internal research center wishes to broach the same topic. If the subject is accepted, control of research instruments is maintained in determining whether the data gathered go beyond the problems originally stated. If they do, then the instruments have to be adjusted.

Certain research issues are prohibited according to the expressed wishes of the prison authorities. These topics include the practical implementation by the prison administration of the rights of convicts during incarceration, any activity by the prison administration to expand the legal rights of inmates, the conditions of confinement and the opinions of the prisoners on this subject, the way in which the inmates are treated by the staff, the welfare of prisoners, their attitude to the staff and fellow prisoners, and the expectations of convicts regarding the prison administration.[15] Outsiders thus are doomed to use mainly the information about prisons propagated by the prison staff's own researchers.

Science of course is protected against the absence of objectivity by the public character of the scientific method.[16] Anyone willing to do so can repeat or test another scholar's research. From this point of view, the knowledge gathered by research centers established by the prison system enjoys the status of *proposed* truths as long as other scholars are deprived of the opportunity of an unhampered examination of the findings. It is true that various institutions, such as scientific periodicals and congresses, have been created to uphold scientific objectivity and criticism. But political power, when it stifles free criticism or fails to protect it, can weaken those institutions. That is true above all in relation to knowledge about those institutions such as prisons which realize the political functions of the political system, particularly a totalitarian one.[17]

Upon entering the penal "sacred area" that is so inaccessible to the "profane," the unwelcome scholar becomes an unwilling part of the political system, always sensitive to scientific criticism. Moreover, awareness of the obstacles and difficulties to be encountered forms an enormous psychological burden and creates an additional subjective barrier to institutional research.

2.

Prison Paranoia

A Pyramidal Organization

In the words of article 2 of Poland's prison staff law of 1959, the staff is "a formation that is monolithic, armed, and in uniform." In other words, it has a paramilitary character and is organized like an army, with a hierarchy of ranks from private to general.[1]

One can distinguish elements of this decidedly hierarchical structure. The work of the prison system is directed by the Central Administration of Penal Institutions, whose head, a general of the prison staff, holds the post of vice-minister of justice. Basic units, such as prisons and detention centers, are located throughout the country. They are divided into regions and are controlled by regional authorities under a Regional Administration of Penal Institutions.[2]

The structure of both of the higher levels reflects the structure of the basic units. For instance, the Central Administration is composed of several organizational units: the organizational-legal department, the staff department, the penitentiary department, the security and command department, the employment and records department, the department of technology and communication, and the health service inspector. Similarly, detention centers and penal institutions have a penitentiary department, a security and command department, a department of employment and records, a financial department, an economic department, and a health service.

The penal institutions and detention centers can also establish independent and group posts for undertaking certain tasks: political, training, social, economic and labor, safety and hygiene.[3] In addition, the penal institutions may include auxiliary economic units, "budget enterprises" (small factories supported by the prison budget), schools, and hospitals.[4]

The penitentiary administration oversees four functions: confinement, social, economic, and resocialization.[5] The implementation of these functions is the duty of special departments of the prison staffs.

The confinement function imposes rules of conduct on convicts so they will conform to the formal aims of the institution. Though all members of the prison staff help fulfill this task, the department of security and command is mainly responsible for security in the institutions and for the observance of regulations, discipline, and order by both inmates and functionaries. It is this department that fulfills the role of prison militia. Security is achieved by placing prisoners in isolation in a separate area with suitable buildings and a system of protection, enforcing discipline, performing searches, preventing escapes and revolts, using safety measures, and meting out stipulated punishments, such as the "hard bed," food rations, solitary confinement, prohibition of smoking, and exclusion from participation in cultural-educational activities.[6]

The social function is a by-product of the confinement function. Because the penitentiary isolates, it takes on full responsibility for the inmates and therefore must guarantee at least minimal living conditions, food, hygiene, and clothing.[7] Carrying out this function is the work of all the departments, but the economic department and health service are chiefly responsible.

The economic function involves compulsory employment of offenders, both in the prisons and in outside enterprises. The system provides general and vocational schooling for inmates to meet the needs of its enterprises.[8] This function is the concern of the civilian employees of the prison enterprises, the school, and above all the department of employment and records, the main manager in the employment of inmates. The tasks of this department also include overseeing the admission and release of inmates, protecting deposited objects, and housing prisoners.[9] This function also is intended to guarantee suitable management of the part of the national wealth at the disposal of the institution, i.e., investment, repair and maintenance, and bookkeeping and supplies.[10] These tasks belong mainly to the economic and financial departments.

The resocialization function is the responsibility of the penitentiary department. Of greatest importance here is the discipline of inmates. This involves a strict regulation of the inmates' behavior toward the prison staff and other prisoners, both in workplaces and in other permitted areas.[11]

The paramilitary character of the prison staff comes with the adoption of hierarchical subordination as a style proper for managing an institution. The system is centralized. It does not exclude handing over power to the lower ranks, but the transfer is carried out according to strict regulations that enable those in higher positions to make decisions "upward" or "downward." The resultant dependence of the lower ranks on their superiors indicates that this hierarchical subordination actually presumes a division of labor and not of competence.

The penal institution is directed by a warden, who is responsible for the realization of all four functions of the prison. All the other functionaries employed in the institution are his subordinates. Hierarchical subordination is obligatory in the management of the penal institution and the whole prison system. The warden has deputies, each of whom is assigned a separate set of duties. The work of particular departments is overseen by directors assisted by deputies. The workers of the departments are subordinate to the directors. The wardens are responsible for tasks entrusted to them and, if it is included in their duties, for a given group of prisoners.[12]

The duties of each functionary of the prison staff are precisely delineated,[13] each responsible for duties assigned to them.[14] This obliges them to an absolute execution of directives issued by the superior organ, with no right to question their correctness, and accountability for failure to carry them out. Even an instruction of a facultative nature, given in the form of a directive or advice, becomes binding, since there is a certain risk and responsibility for what might happen should that advice not be taken into consideration. The system of hierarchic subordination usually adopts the method of directive management.[15]

The higher the post in the official hierarchy a functionary holds, the greater the responsibility. A characteristic feature of the organization of the prison staff is the fact that the superior is held responsible for the work of his subordinates. The greatest responsibility therefore lies with the warden of the penal institution.

The warden is the direct head of the institution.[16] He divides tasks among his personnel, is responsible for administering punishment in accordance with the principles of the penitentiary policy, and molds the life of the institution and the situation of its inmates. The burden of responsibility placed upon the warden for his own activity or that of his personnel, and for the results of the didactic process determines his position as a superior of the functionaries employed in the institution and as the superior of its inmates.[17]

He directs all the departments of the staff, constantly controls them, and is responsible for his own and his subordinates' activities. . . . He is personally responsible for peace and order in the prison, for the strict carrying out of instructions and decisions of the authorities, and for administering punishments in accordance with the binding regulations. . . . He is obliged to take care of the rational organization, from the didactic and income point of view, of the prisoners' work, school, and other forms of training, the sanitary state of the prison, the health of the inmates, proper feeding, clothes, and bedding. He has the right to mete out penalties, within the limits of binding regulations, to subordinate staff and to the prisoners. The warden of the prison can issue regulations in important and urgent cases which transcend the range of his rights.[18]

In turn, the deputies of the warden and the heads of particular services are responsible for their subordinates and for the duties they perform.[19] Lower staff members are responsible for the proper fulfillment of their own duties and those of the functionaries subordinate to them. If they work with prisoners, they are responsible for the group of inmates under them.[20] Responsibilities of staff members therefore increase correspondingly with the rank of their official post.

Prison rules foresee punishment of inmates for misdemeanors,[21] and official staff regulations foresee penalties for functionaries.[22] A prisoner's misconduct is analyzed not only from the point of view of its importance and the suitable punishment but also according to whether the fault lies with a specific functionary, who perhaps ignored his obligations and made the wrongdoing possible. If, for instance, a fight breaks out among inmates in the exercise yard during the absence of functionaries who should have been with the inmates, the functionaries must be punished along with the inmates. Of course, the absence of staff members during such an incident can also testify unfavorably about the work of their superiors.

In such a situation, a violation of prison staff rules can of course be registered only if it is detected by a superior or if a functionary who is not directly responsible for the given group of prisoners notifies the superiors of the institution. One cannot rely on the possibility that the surveillance in the exercise yard will of their own accord inform the warden about neglecting their duties.

A formal notification about a misdemeanor to the superiors or the warden obliges them or him to take certain steps against all those responsible for the event, including inmates, functionaries, and direct superiors. If, however, the person who notifies the warden about the violation is the superior himself, he places himself in a favorable situation; he noticed the misbehavior and thus was alert, a good worker. To a certain extent, the informer can become the executor of the sanctions placed on the function-aries. If the guards notice misbehaving prisoners and stop a fight, then only the participants in the fight will be penalized. In that situation there is no misdemeanor on the part of the staff, who were on the spot and re-acted suitably; the chain of punishments is broken at the prisoners' stage. But if the guards find out about the fight after it occurs they may well re-main silent and count on the secrecy of others.

The functionaries may be found guilty of much more serious misde-meanors:

> Let us say that a prisoner has been beaten and, to make it impossible for him to demand an official medical examination, he was placed by the guards re-sponsible for the assault in solitary confinement. In this cell, still beaten or threatened with further violence and starved, he took his life. This event is serious enough so that its disclosure . . . could signify not only certain con-sequences in relation to the direct perpetrators but also to their superiors and the warden, and it testifies unfavorably about the work of the prison system. The case would have to involve the prosecutor, who would bring an accu-sation against the direct perpetrators. The charges of negligence of duties would spread to consecutive superiors, including the warden, and quite pos-sibly the examination would also concern the eventual responsibility of the appropriate Regional Administration of Penal Institutions—for example, whether prior controls had been put in place in the institution. . . .[23]

The prisoners constitute the base of a pyramid whose particular stages of responsibility lead to the pinnacle—to the warden, who is responsible for the whole prison. No one is subordinate to the prisoners, and there are no persons for whom they can be held responsible. The lack of such re-sponsibility demonstrates their nonparticipation in power. The entire day of the subordinates of these total institutions is planned; the same is true of the ways of satisfying their fundamental needs. In other words, as Goffman pointed out, total institutions take over responsibility for the sub-ordinates and must secure for them everything that is regarded as indispensable.[24]

The Conspiracy of Ignorance

Each level of the prison system, when threatened with dire conse-quences, will try if possible to endow the precipitating event with an official interpretation that helps those involved avoid being held responsible. Superiors will intentionally ignore the efforts of their staff, preparing their own version of an incident by, for example, persuading the inmate witnesses to make false statements or forcing them to do so.[25] Events that leave no material traces but testify negatively about the work of the superiors, such as the drunkenness of functionaries while on duty, may be "forgotten" by the superiors unless they are officially informed about such misbehavior. By being silent, however, a person faces the threat that his behavior may be brought to the attention of superiors and result in additional consequences.

The unwillingness of superiors to be officially informed about incidents perpetrated by their own subordinates or a silent agreement to prepare a suitable official version of events to avoid disclosure at a higher level constitutes what I term *avoidance of negative knowledge*. The universal avoidance of negative knowledge by a sizable group of functionaries I call *generalization of the avoidance of negative knowledge*. Thus this term takes into account the place in the official hierarchy of the prison staff threatened with official consequences as a result of the obligation to officially disclose an incident to higher ups. Hiding knowledge about the avoidance of negative knowledge I call a *conspiracy of ignorance*. Such a conspiracy obviously is a defensive measure against the pyramidally organized responsibility system, whose essence is that higher ups can be held responsible for certain behaviors of other members of the organization as well as for their consequences.

The upshot of the whole system is that (1) slight misdemeanors, for which responsibility is not transferred to others or is transferred only to a small degree, are more likely to be revealed than are infractions for which the responsibility falls on people who are not their direct perpetrators, and (2) the less the probability of disclosure of the misdemeanor, the greater the number of persons who could be held responsible and the higher their place in the hierarchy.

The Statistical Dangers

If the staff of a prison are able to meet the expectations of superiors at a level higher than their own institution, the evaluation of the work of the penitentiary units and their wardens will be heightened. This evaluation is made on the basis of information supplied by the warden to the central institution. In other words, the warden is judged by his superiors on the basis of his own information about the implementation of orders and not on the basis of their actual realization. That means the warden can conduct his own private penitentiary policy.

The nature and number of misdemeanors committed by functionaries is one of the most important bases for the authorities of a penal institution and, above all, the regional and central authorities to estimate the discipline of the prison staff. This estimation is made by comparing data from other institutions. A hierarchical list of penal institutions in particular regions according to the number of their misdeeds is then composed. The listing is important for the division of rewards and bonuses among the regions and institutions. It is also relevant in shaping a personnel policy.

Under these circumstances, it is easy to see why prison staffs are interested in keeping the number of misdemeanors low. Staffs are most concerned with creating the best possible picture of the personnel, their morale, their qualifications, and so on. Consequently, the prison report introduces distinguished staff members and those of merit, displays an institution's achievements and photographs of the best employees, and in general describes the institution in the best possible terms.

The warden does not like it when he receives a formal notification about misconduct committed by a staff member, for such a report leaves a trace in the documents, while he himself is obliged to take a stand in the case. Notification is also disliked by department heads, counselors, and wardens, since a serious misdeed committed by an inmate throws a shadow on their work.

Comparison with other penitentiary units means that statistics can become dangerous. The same peril exists when comparisons are made on the basis of data from the same institution but for different years. This danger is mitigated with the aid of secret projects to limit the number of reported misdemeanors. Such projects assume that the institution will remain as close as possible to the predicted median for all institutions and that the misdemeanor index for an institution will not deteriorate. All events that might eventually affect the index negatively will be suitably sanitized in accordance with the rule of avoiding negative knowledge.

The power to disclose or hide negative events within the framework of the plan is a dangerous tool in the hands of the heads of penal institutions. The absence of clear-cut criteria for reporting or hiding misconduct intensifies the feeling of uncertainty and menace generated by the existence of informal channels of information.

Mutual Capture

Because no staff member is interested in giving formal notification to the warden of misdemeanors committed by employees, such notifications are made only when the misdemeanors cannot be ignored. Usually they are made by staff members of one department about those in another, frequently as the result of conflicts between departments. Most often the conflicts involve members of the security department.

The tendency to conceal misdeeds of staff members raises the possibility that management might lose control of the situation in a prison. To avoid that, informal channels of information are developed. What officially is not seen nor heard becomes unofficially the object of intense efforts to know about everything happening in an institution. The administration organizes for itself an inflow of information from trusties in menial positions and from prisoners about both the work of the staff and the behavior of other inmates. The administration tries to give the impression that it knows everything. When it unofficially informs workers about their misdeeds (which they believed had not come to light), it heightens the impression that it knows everything and hears everything. The employees may become convinced that the walls have ears.

An informer's job offered by the warden or some other higher up to an employee can be a form of distinction. A refusal to act as an informer is not well received and places the person who refuses outside the group of trusties, lowering his chances for promotion. A worker or inmate may become a voluntary "squealer" if he is "spotted" for drunkenness, theft, unexcused absence, or some neglect of duties. Informing in such situations is seen by the superior as a form of rehabilitation. When unofficially informed about a functionary's infringement, the superior may, depending on needs, turn it into an official case. If the incident testifies negatively about the work of a superior, he will probably pass over it in silence. That is not to say he will forget about it.

The informal information system implies in turn an informal system of punishments and rewards. A known but undisclosed violation may become the cause for informal punishment of the perpetrator: additional work hours, voluntary (unpaid) work, no advancement in pay, lack of promotion, a dressing down in private, assignment to unattractive tasks, or a change of posts.

These informal systems of information gathering and of penalties and rewards make for mutual relations among employees that are dominated by uncertainty and distrust.[26] The functionaries seek to eliminate the consequent feelings of threat and insecurity in three main ways.

Some functionaries assume the pose of eager workers when they are around those whom they distrust, including fellow workers and strangers. The rule is that one should never behave in such a way as to enable someone else to "have something" on one; that would be like handing weapons to the enemy. The situation in which one "has nothing" on another person, even if mutual, offers no feeling of security in the presence of the other. The considerable risk of behaving in a way contrary to regulations makes the other person a potential inconvenient witness. Everyone seeks information harmful to other persons, something that can be passed on to superiors to hurt others' reputations. The chief aim is not necessarily to harm another but to have something on him, a good weapon which at the same time convinces one that the other person is no better than oneself. But this weapon is not used needlessly. If it were, one might deprive oneself of something that protects. Moreover, informing might encourage others to view one as a squealer. This weapon is usually simply held rather than employed; its function consists mainly in making the interested parties realize that one possesses it.

A second way of eliminating feelings of insecurity is to try not to cross the path of a person who has something on one. One may be ill treated, ignored, or spoken badly about and not react directly, since one can be harmed. That is why information about those who can harm one is specially sought after. If this task proves impossible, it becomes necessary to spread information that could harm the other.

The third way arises when two persons have something on each other. On this basis they can build mutual trust, become friends, and feel free in each other's company. An acquaintanceship that does not include such a mutual acknowledgment of "sins" is worth little. This equilibrium eliminates uncertainty in relations with others and is in fact a model for which the whole inmate community strives to follow. The two "partners" arrange their relations with others so as not to endanger the mutual trust.

Even prison interactions based on such trust differ, however, from relations shared by "free" people. If non-inmates maintain contacts with a person it is usually because they like him and have a high regard for his conduct. They try to act so as not to offend the other person. This interaction seems to be based on an element of control—the effort to act in accordance with certain values. That element is absent from the prison model of interaction, and the mutual "I have something on someone" opens possibilities of acting without being hampered by the other person, contrary to those highly regarded values. A member of the prison community concentrates on detecting something bad in another person. He does not like someone who has a clean slate, and it is particularly bad if such a person has something on somebody else. He must then hunt for some misfortune of the other and incessantly try to prove that he is no better than anyone else. The successive consequences of such a downward trend are that one believes more in damaging than in positive information.

To become informed one must not only organize an inflow of information; one has to provide information, too. In this way, networks for gaining and transmitting deprecatory information appear. If one wishes to harm others, one can send via these networks false information which, despite lack of proof, is easily believed. It is said that "every piece of gossip contains some truth." The networks thereby produce a "black" picture of a functionary as a drunkard, a thief, an informer. Any coarse behavior or infringement of regulations by the staff member is widely talked about. As a result, other staff become convinced of the worst behavior of their colleagues and in the process enjoy a certain feeling of being better than the other. The vicious circle closes. By only striving not to be worse than others, one lowers one's own moral standards, permitting oneself to indulge in unsuitable behavior. The picture of the "generalized other" produced by the community of functionaries is sufficiently negative that everyone sees themselves in a more favorable light.[27]

In this manner the configuration of relations stabilizes if one has something on everyone else, while one's vision of the other is lowered to such a level of "worseness" that eventually what the other has on oneself ceases to be dangerous. The term *mutual capture* probably expresses most aptly such relations within the prison community.

A World of Secrets

Let us imagine that someone steals a large sum of money. Happy that his undertaking was successful, he boasts about his venture to his friends.

His joy, however, proves short-lived—the "friends" steal his money and our thief finds himself in a strange situation. Although he knows who took the money, he cannot seek legal assistance—the money, after all, was gained by means of a crime. He also cannot rely on a voluntary return of the sum—his demands would simply be ignored. The "friends" assume correctly that he will not be a fool and notify the police; if he did, he could be charged himself. Our thief knows that he cannot harm his "friends" without bringing trouble upon himself, and he is aware that they too know this. To act sensibly he must keep the whole matter secret, and in this respect he can certainly depend on reciprocity. With this assurance, he can try to regain the money by, for example, organizing a group of persons who will force the new owners to return it, or who will at least punish them severely.

There are of course many ways of behaving in such a situation. I wish to emphasize at this stage that what occurred between the thief and his pals will remain secret, presuming they all act wisely.[28] The whole event could set into motion a further course of interactions which also remain secret. None of the parties involved will seek legal methods to end the conflict but, wishing to resolve it, will open ways for a multiplication of concealed facts. This type of event produces a new social reality in which the interested parties will not strive to regulate it by means of legal rules. They will enact certain codes of behavior in various types of secret interactions.

The person who initiates secret interactions must have a guarantee or be assured that the partner will keep secret the information or behavior which he witnessed. Disclosure could bring upon the perpetrator suitable punishment administered by persons or institutions motivated or obligated to do so. The sanctions result in loss of that with which the perpetrator was most concerned. They may take the form of emotional, moral, legal, economic, physical, or other penalties. It is precisely the threat of punishment that makes the partners' silence so necessary. Trust in the tacit interaction has its source in the sanction which the participants can apply against each other for violating the secret.

In such secret interactions the partners retain an awareness that their contents cannot be disclosed; others cannot learn anything about them. It is only because there exists a world of people who should not know that it becomes necessary to differentiate events into those which can be disclosed and those to be kept secret—negative knowledge. This is feasible because of familiarity with society and the rules obligatory within it; this type of knowledge is also necessary to make one's behavior correspond to eventual consequences. The initiation of secret interactions also imposes a knowledge about the types of bonds linking one with one's partners and the sorts of interactions one can employ in relation to them. All this endows the secret interaction with the appearance of a conscious experience. Secret interactions do not have to take place as a result of the good will of their participants if they are based on the mutual possession of negative knowledge about each other. They also eliminate the element of social control typical in other interactions. In this particular interaction one does not have to be as constrained with one's partner as in other interactions; the partner is not dangerous, and one does not need to feel ashamed in front of him as one does in the presence of others. But the elimination of social control from the secret interaction is conducive to the production of negative events that may disrupt the legal order.

It is precisely toward this type of interaction, involving the greatest possible number of persons so as to reduce the feeling of threat, that members of the prison community strive. Such secret interactions in the institution eliminate other relations, planned and expressed in formal regulations, into which members of the institution should enter. Actually, legal regulations play a limited role in steering the life of these institutions. Secret interactions appear among both the superiors and the subordinates. The universal nature of these secret interactions may for all practical purposes actually abolish the official hierarchy, leading to the deterioration of formal authority.

The abrogated regulations and formal hierarchy are replaced by a new social structure, produced within secret interactions. Because these interactions are secret, this new structure, in contrast to the formal one, is not wholly known to members of the institution. But it features new social events with specific, normative codes that do not refer to the official ones. That is how secret interactions create a field for new social facts and a new normative order that regulates the new social events.

I call this new order the secret life of a prison. Its essential feature for the investigator is social solidarity. Because no one exists or has a chance to live without his faults being known to others, no one is able to talk about his own misconduct. Disclosure of even a small fragment could end with disclosure of the whole, which would be greatly unprofitable for everyone concerned. And so the appearance of someone new, including an academic investigator, means that the community must know what role to play in front of this new person.

The Facade of Formal Organization

Examination of a penitentiary requires an awareness of the dangers that could disturb or interrupt the process of becoming acquainted with this reality. Individuals who create a certain community are more or less conscious that they could be examined. The investigator also cannot remain indifferent to the attitude toward being examined which is taken by members of the community. It has been argued that the investigated reality can be so transformed by the research process that it becomes impossible to achieve reliable results. That often does occur because of the subjects' awareness of being examined and their accompanying attitudes. In the social sciences the causal chain simply does not exist in the social sphere without consciousness.[29] The human subject can, after all, consciously decipher from the investigator the truth about himself or lie to make the investigator err. No research object except a person can in such an independent way explain or conceal itself from an investigator, since no other object modifies its behavior once it becomes known.[30] Thus the investigator should remain aware of the fact that the discernible presence of a stranger in a community can alter it. He or she also should keep in mind that even though the community becomes accustomed to his or her presence, it can change again when another stranger appears.

Experience teaches us that when we arrive for the first time at the home of new acquaintances, the meeting is rather ceremonious. We know very well that the everyday life of that household is quite different. We assume that a new social reality presents itself as different than it actually is. In addition, the person making our acquaintance, as a rule, wants us to believe that he possesses all the traits which he wishes to possess, that what he does will produce effects in accordance with his earlier declared intention, and that generally things are as he presents them. People create facades that define a situation while often concealing the gap between the illusions upheld and reality.[31]

The illusions which reflect official values are attempts at playing such idealized roles. The pictures of the ideal roles of members of the institution are in fact components of its formal organization, a scheme of behavior and relations that is intentionally planned for its members within the framework of appropriate privileges.[32] To see this we do not have to carry out any research. The formal organization is after all composed of an official hierarchy defined on paper as an organizational scheme with instructions on how to act.[33] Instead of visiting the prison it would be enough to purchase several legal books to find out what official life in prison is like.

In a penitentiary, the behavior of the investigator is judged more or less consciously from the point of view of whether it serves the observer's purposes. There exists the incessant wish to penetrate the investigator's mind to discover what he or she knows and plans to do. The inmates and particularly the staff members want to control the state of the investigator's knowledge and attitudes toward the reality found in prison. The direct disclosure by the investigator of his intentions can set into motion acts on the part of the community that will block the realization of his plans, or the community may present itself in such a form that the investigator has to question the adequacy of information collected on such a basis.

That is often the case with brief visits by people from the outside. In one penal institution for mentally defective women and prisoners with personality problems, visiting foreigners were shown three cells to acquaint them with living conditions.[34] In the first cell all the inmates were smoking cigarettes (which is strictly forbidden) and sat in various places, including on the bed (which is also not allowed). The overall impression was that the inmates enjoyed considerable freedom. In the second cell the inmates sat at a table looking at a cake; this was supposed to suggest a homelike atmosphere. In the third cell two of the inmates were sitting at a table with a chessboard. For anyone even slightly familiar with the reality of prison life, these scenes seemed artificial and stage managed. The inmates were visibly nervous and seemed concerned about how well they were playing their assigned roles. But the whole incident was not untypical of the way prisons seek to present themselves to outsiders.

3.

Learning from the Failure of Previous Studies

The Defensive Measures of a Paranoid

Investigators wishing to visit a penal institution usually plan to stay for a relatively short period even though they intend to examine a large number of people. They imagine, for instance, that there should be little difficulty in organizing a sizable group of inmates for a survey in a penal institution and that there should be no problems in finding a place to conduct such research. After all, the warden or counselor has only to summon successive groups to the recreation hall, and in a short time the research will be completed. It appears to be simple, but in reality the situation is quite the reverse. For example, the impression left by any earlier investigators will directly influence the attitudes of the inmates and staff toward all future research. When a penal community has little or no previous research experience, the inmates and functionaries behave with great reserve during the initial stage. They are unwilling to begin conversations, and they keep their distance. In the presence of an investigator they behave very formally, both toward him and toward their peers.[1]

Distrust and suspicion can be manifested by the functionaries' attempts to prevent the investigator's learning about negative aspects of the institution. During my own research, this was accomplished in various ways:

Interviews with the inmates had to take place in the presence of the functionaries. The excuse was that they were responsible for the safety of the visitors.

• The respondents (the inmates) could not be chosen at random. The same arguments were used as above: "Some of the prisoners are very aggressive and it is difficult to predict what they would do." It was proposed that the inmates be chosen by the staff on duty that day.

• The course of the research was controlled and its "true purpose" was tested by sending in prisoner-informers:

1. If it were agreed that interviews with the prisoners be held without the presence of functionaries, there had to be at least two inmates at the interviews. Usually these were not close acquaintances, and each one was afraid to speak to the other.

2. Purposeful disinformation was accomplished by summoning, in addition to informants, those prisoners who were soon to be released, or had obtained conditional release (or were trying to receive it), as well as those who in the eyes of the prison staff were well behaved. Any of these had something to lose if it were discovered that they relayed unfavorable information about the work of the administration.

3. Difficulties were encountered when aggressive, noisy, or mentally retarded prisoners were selected, or when delays occurred in summoning the inmates.

Investigator Y conducted experimental research[2] and at first managed quite well. But at a certain stage in the course of a successive interview she ran out into the corridor and turned to the counselors for help in completing the interview. She claimed that for some time she was unable to cope with the inmates. She was exasperated by their behavior and feared that the results of the research were no longer a function of the controlled experiment but of the "antics" of the inmates. After the intervention of the counselors, the investigations were continued without further incidents, but Y was no longer satisfied with the outcome and suspected that it was rather the effect of the intentional behavior of the prisoners since regular patterns were absent.

I experienced another situation.[3] I arrived at the prison and for several days I was forbidden to administer a questionnaire. Finally, I was granted permission to start my work on a Sunday in January at about 6 p.m. The cell block in which the research was to be conducted was a corridor about 50 yards long. Along one wall of the corridor were doors to the cells. About 250 inmates were housed here with only one functionary—a guard who assigned the recreation hall for the interviews and successively escorted the prisoners. After each group of prisoners entered, the guard closed the door from the outside and departed to pursue his other duties— leaving me quite alone with the inmates. There was no possibility of opening the door from the inside. Only after prolonged knocking would the guard open it and usher in the next prisoners.

Research with the first group went quite peacefully and only one of the prisoners declined to complete the questionnaire, claiming that he was illiterate. After a few minutes the lights went out. This gave rise to laughter and shouts and the inmates exchanged comments. They left their seats and walked around the room. A moment later the lights went on and the prisoners continued filling out the questionnaires. The guard glanced through the slightly opened door and once again locked us in from the outside. This group was immediately followed by another which was composed of seven men. All were strangely excited and aggressive. "Where are you from," they asked. "From Warsaw," I answered. " . . . he's a local." "And who are you?" I asked. "I'm a code user" [one who uses the prison argot]. "My old lady is one, and so is sis. The whole family uses the code." Slightly nervous I managed to induce the prisoners to sit down and showed them the instructions. There were no questions. The lights went off and the prisoners began to scream and laugh wildly. They abandoned their seats, went up to the windows, and shouted something toward the street. They surrounded me, brushing against me and knocking my bag off the table. Now they were much more excited than at the beginning of the interview. They also provoked me to talk: "Do you have a piece of ass?" "Yes, I do." "Do you fuck her?" "Of course." "What do you do?" "I am studying." "Then you'll become a reptile" [a pejorative term used for describing the prison staff]. "No, I won't." But the tension in the room was growing, not dissipating. The lights didn't go on and no one came in. Of course, I was quite afraid and wondered whether or not to throw myself against the door, and begin hammering with my fists and shouting so that I could escape the "bandits" (I thought in those terms) who continued to brush against me asking me insulting and provocative questions.

"Do you know how the girls do it in the women's [prison]?" "No, I don't but tell me, it interests me." Laughter. "Of course, who isn't interested?" They began their story, admiring it themselves and awakening my authentic shock and interest. They described how the women inmates inserted boiled sweets into the vagina and then "licked it for each other," about the porridge from their supper placed inside a stocking and sewn up in such a way as to form something resembling a "stiff and warm" male organ with which they masturbated each other. The inmates knew all this from the girls who "sat" and who practiced these activities.

They also described a rape committed by up to twenty women inmates on a male prisoner. Having discovered him in the attic of one of the prison buildings, they first sent the prettiest girl to carry out the foreplay. Then the others threw themselves on him, tying his penis so as to stop the flow of blood and performed intercourse. The rape victim was injured and needed medical attention. The inmates also told me about sexual relations between the male personnel in the women's prisons and the inmates. These tales about sex relaxed my interlocutors to such an extent that they changed their attitude toward me and I even won their sympathy. They now addressed me as "sir," and politely without hostility asked what I would like to know. This was much better. I asked that they continue the theme they had begun.

Anxiety and tension had disappeared and the meeting changed into a general conversation—no one was nervously walking around the room. The prisoners inquired about the situation "outside," the possibility of an amnesty, etc.; they also admitted that the guard had instructed them to frighten me off. Finally, the lights went on. When the guard came back, I said goodbye to the inmates, promising that we would meet again. I also informed the functionary that the light was faulty and I was unable to conduct my work, thanked him, and departed.

Other obstacles created by the functionaries include:

• Severe treatment of those prisoners invited to take part in the research. Sometimes they were instructed how to behave: "Don't say anything stupid, you know what I mean."

• The functionaries, without being asked, divulged information about life in the penal institution: "Here the prisoners have it cozy . . . just like at home. . . . They have everything and are satisfied. . . . Most didn't have it this good outside the prison."

• Hostility toward certain inmates was encouraged by showing or describing documents detailing murders, rape, and other particularly cruel crimes.

The suspicion and animosity of the prisoners was expressed in the following behavior:

• Some did not shake hands although the investigator extended his. Those inmates who did shake hands said magic words right away to annul this form of contact with an "unclean" person.

• The prisoners called the investigators "reptilian seed," i.e., people who were planning to work in the penal or judicial system. Prison employees were known as "reptiles," students were "reptilian seed." We were also described as "red spiders," that is, we were taken for party members, communists, or their coworkers.

• Sometimes the inmates refused to participate in research or gave "polite" answers: "I don't complain," "I have nothing against anyone."

• At other times they expressed their animosity maintaining that "nothing improves for us in prison as a result of these studies . . . and they even think up worse things for us—all those changes in the rules."

• Some of the inmates checked whether or not I was passing the information to the functionaries.

During the first meeting one of the inmates didn't want to talk. Instead, he asked me to look at the two solitary confinement cells which he described as terrible. He also told me where to find them and proposed to meet once again. I saw the two identical cells: cold spaces in the corner of which was a cement perpendicular block on which lay a wooden lattice of the sort used in showers in public baths together with a wooden head rest—this was the sleeping area. In the middle of the cells stood a cement table on a single leg (which came out of the cement floor) and next to it a cement stool. In the corner a wide pipe stuck out of the wall, intended as the toilet.

A few days later I met with the same inmate and told him that I had seen the cells. He in turn described numerous drastic events connected with solitary confinement. He also explained why he did not want to say all this earlier. First, he had checked whether or not I would inform the staff about the fact that he had mentioned the cells. Had I done so, he would have been punished "but only slightly, because this information . . . was not a big deal." Since he hadn't suffered any sanctions, he concluded that I was "alright" and he could talk "openly."

As long as the investigator doesn't antagonize the inmates and staff, this first difficult period soon passes. The change can be noted when the functionaries abandon certain restrictions; for example, we were permitted to freely choose persons for purposes of study, or to talk alone with a single inmate. The second stage was characterized by increased interest of the prisoners and staff in the persons conducting the studies. At the same time, a singular competition began between the inmates and the personnel for establishing better relations with us. The inmates would tell us how badly they were treated by the administration of the institution. The functionaries, in turn, would describe the criminal acts committed by the inmates, drawing particular attention to the degeneration of the perpetrators. They claimed that the prisoners are "lazy good-for-nothings, whom the state has to keep" while they (the staff) have to "suffer with them."

During the second stage symptoms of distrust present in the first period gradually disappeared. Both the inmates and the staff more eagerly established rapport, and in the third stage expressed a readiness to become friendly and confess. As a rule, members of both groups took the initiative to be on first-name terms. It became attractive to be associated with the newcomer, and being seen in his company became a source of satisfaction. The functionaries almost always accompanied persons conducting the studies, making it difficult to carry out work and out-right impossible to talk with the inmates.

The Closed Circuit of Information

The inmates (and to a certain degree also the functionaries) spend a good part of their lives in one place—the prison. Their work and lives are a duplication of an unchanging, universally familiar routine. Anything new or different immediately becomes a subject of discussion. But these new events are not as frequent as outside the prison walls. It could be said that there is a certain deficiency of information and a longing that something will happen. One boasts of possessing information and no matter what the content or the source, anyone who has some news is the subject of immediate and special interest. In prisons it is said: "Nothing can be kept secret here for very long." Information is passed on secretly or in the open. As a result, in a very short time everyone knows everything about the given event including the interpretations added on the way. This is a *closed circuit of information*. If a certain group of inmates is randomly selected for a study, after having talked with some of them, on the very same day all the other inmates know that such research is being conducted and its purpose, and they are already predisposed toward our work. The next persons interviewed are no longer "the same" as the first few. Interpretations of the research by the inmate community will influence whether, for example, an inmate will refuse to participate or not, the sort of answers he will give, etc. Each consecutive event connected with the research will become common knowledge and will reflect on the attitude of the successive persons concerned.

X carried out a survey[4] in which he asked the prisoners to mark on a scale their opinion about the situations described in the questionnaire. These situations were "scenes" from prison life. The guard escorted randomly selected prisoners in groups of ten—there were ten tables, one for each inmate, and there was no possibility for communication between the respondents. After one set of the inmates completed the questionnaire, the next ten entered according to a list of selected names. But during the successive change of groups the investigator realized that since the last two groups, prisoners had been marking identical opinions and in such places on the scale that it was obvious that they had heard nothing about these events, knew nothing, or that nothing of the sort had ever occurred in their institution.

The following three groups behaved in the same manner. X began to despair and was ready to give up on this study. It would seem that the more neutral the contents of the studies, and more distant from prison life, the less probable that their interpretation by the inmates would significantly influence the results of the studies. If the purpose of the survey was "hidden life," then it was necessary to take into consideration a more frequent than usual refusal to participate as well as intentionally false answers. Such disinformation could be fostered both by the heads of "hidden life" and by the staff. This particular example was an excellent illustration of the impact of research upon the results. Apart from whether the situations described in the "scenes" did or did not take place in the community of the inmates, the very examination of "hidden life" constituted a challenge mainly to the most privileged groups in the informal structure of the prisoners' community to see whether they would keep silent with regard to matters of which a stranger should remain ignorant. After testing the first group of inmates the information about the contents of the interviews had already spread throughout the prison. The investigations were interpreted as an attempt to penetrate the problems of those groups. The inmates decided to negate the statements in the survey regardless of their veracity. They created an atmosphere of ridicule surrounding the investigation. Some of the inmates carefully observed the way in which prisoners who did not belong to the privileged groups marked their answers. On the second day the respondents completed the survey ten minutes earlier, did not ask for instructions to be repeated, had no questions, and did not have to be told to sit singly at the tables—they did so by themselves immediately after entering the recreation hall. This gave the impression that before they arrived they knew exactly what their tasks would consist of. Some of the inmates refused to participate even before entering the hall.

In conversations with me after the research, the prisoners claimed that the survey was not anonymous. I was surprised to hear this, considering that the inmates were only requested to circle or check their attitude to the described situations and nothing else—no names, age, or origin—was demanded. The inmates nonetheless maintained that it is possible to recreate precisely who completed which questionnaire by remembering the place where he sat, the color of his ink, or the order in which the questionnaire was completed, and that with the help of the guards who escorted the inmates to the hall one could determine their names. They would have been happier not to participate at all, but a general refusal could be badly viewed by the administration and the inmates wanted to avoid this. The best solution would be to come and prove that no one knows anything. Then, they would have no further problems and would unanimously state that there are no elements of "hidden life" such as those presented in the survey. If in a conversation with one of the inmates I would say that it was general knowledge that the prisoners of this particular institution were divided, and that events occur which are the outcome of this division, his answer could usually be summed up: everyone knows that but proof is quite another matter.

It was the contention of the inmates that the questionnaires demanded almost a confession about participation in "hidden life" and violated the obligation to keep silent on the subject of essential events in the life of the prisoners. The research, therefore, was a sui generis violent act against the community since its members were unable to refuse to take part. The inmates also believed that such a refusal would be interpreted by the administration as disobedience which, in turn, would reflect badly on the administration. The prisoners were thus forced to take a stand regarding matters which they do not discuss with strangers.

Even more surprising, the inmates regarded conversation with me as something quite different from filling out questionnaires—in contrast to words which can always be contradicted or denied, writing leaves a trace. Even the expression that "a study is being conducted" sounded serious and threatening. The procedure of being summoned, sitting down and filling out questionnaires made it a special event. It was analyzed from the point of view of eventual dire consequences for the persons involved. Anonymity actually suggested that the questions concern dangerous issues. The suspicion that anonymity could be violated without the knowledge and willingness of the inmates meant that they wondered whether some sort of a dishonest game was being played behind their backs.

A face-to-face conversation is different and emphasizes the individuality of the inmate who becomes the center of attention and can speak without fear—words exist as they are uttered and when one finishes speaking, no traces remain. This closed circuit of information and the attitudes of those under examination mean that the behavior of the investigator is important. If the investigators act in ways that humiliate or insult the person under examination, then they can be certain that they have turned the prisoner against them. The other inmates will quickly find out about this conduct and judge the investigators accordingly. If, for example, in the situation cited above (when I found myself alone with the prisoners in a dark room), I had thrown myself against the door and shouted to open it (and this was what fear dictated), I would have had nothing more to do in that particular institution. Furthermore, I would have become the object of mockery and ridicule, and this attitude toward me would certainly have been transferred into the work I conducted.

Proper use of this aspect of the prison community can direct the attitude of the inmates to the research in a favorable direction. Investigators should not divulge what they have found out about the prison either to the staff or to the inmates; even more so, they should never admit who was the source of information or what and whom they have seen. If news starts to spread that the investigator disclosed the contents of interviews, then nothing will be found out in the future or the investigator will be disinformed in further interviews.

At the same time, the prison staff takes care that no one should "sell out the prison." Anyone who does so can expect to be punished. It is true that many of the prisoners talk about the institution without fear of repressions and are prepared to face penalties; they attach little importance to the possibility of, for example, being beaten—for them, they claim, "truth is more important."

On the Sources of Prisoners' Knowledge and Certain Pertinent Problems

Prisoners rarely serve their entire sentence in a single penal institution. They are transferred to other units for various reasons: when a prisoner ceases to be a juvenile offender (over 21) he/she can be shifted to an institution for first offenders; prisoners are moved from overpopulated institutions to the less populated ones; badly behaved inmates are handed over to institutions with a stricter regime; prisoners with five, ten, or more years left to serve are moved to special institutions intended precisely for such terms; certain inmates leave closed institutions for semi-open ones, and so forth.

The inmates "travel," and those "journeys" provide them with knowledge about life in other institutions which is also the subject of exchanged information. This is why each convict has knowledge about the situation in the institution where he had served time, the one where he is currently confined, and those about which he found out from other prisoners while "traveling across the country." An enormous source of information about penal institutions are the recidivists. The older recidivists provide valuable information about the situation in the more distant past. I was able to use their reminiscences while analyzing changes within the "hidden life" in penitentiaries.

Once one overcomes their distrust, the inmates reveal a tendency toward an uncontrolled narrative based on associations. It is difficult to focus their attention on a single theme. Their statements are dominated by descriptions of events and by their own emotional attitudes toward them. Sometimes it is impossible to interrupt or to stop them from talking. Therefore one should collect information while listening to everything the prisoner wants to tell you, and during the following meeting to ask questions, only if the prisoner allows you to do so. This inclination on the part of the inmates is particularly important during the initial stage of research when it is not yet clear what to ask and how to ask it. In this way a lot of information can be gained acquainting the investigator with the customs and social order governing the prisons. But for those very reasons one has to be especially careful in order to extract from the tide of disorderly information what the inmate is talking about, the source of his information, and the period to which it pertains. The inmates like to be listened to carefully. One can steer the topic of their statements by showing greater or lesser interest about the related incidents, thus encouraging them to expand a theme of special interest to the investigator.

Inmates who hold the highest position in the social stratification of the prison are not allowed to speak about the mores of a given institution; otherwise, they could be expelled from their group. For this reason, it is very difficult to obtain any sort of information from them. While organizing an interview, one should take special care to guarantee anonymity and discretion.

In talking with more than one prisoner (or in the presence of other prisoners) one should remember that the divisions of the prison community into groups means that each inmate will speak only about "safe" topics in the presence of an unknown inmate or a member of another group. As a rule, everyone is willing to describe the wrongs suffered by them, often expecting that perhaps the investigator will be able to put them right.

On the Dissimilarity of the World of the Investigator and the World of the Prisoners, and on Other Perils

Investigators who conduct studies in penal institutions should not assume that life in prison is similar to that outside. That which we could expect to be unpleasant for the prisoner does not have to be so and vice versa. For example, a question about the reason for the incarceration is regarded as completely normal, but holiday greetings can come as a total shock. An inquiry whether a woman prisoner has a boyfriend could reduce her to tears. What amuses the inmate can be horrifying to outsiders, and so on.

One of the most dissimilar things is the prisoners' language, full of expressions completely unknown to outsiders or familiar but with a different meaning. It is not embarrassing to inquire about the meaning of various words and expressions, but it can be harmful to use the argot unskillfully. Certain studies have indicated in using the prisoners' vernacular (and sometimes their opinions) a tendency to mimic the inmates. By doing so instead of establishing contact, investigators only make themselves look ridiculous. The inmates are perfectly well aware of the differences, not only in regard to their position, between themselves and the investigator.

It is possible that the researcher could be robbed or the prisoners could try to steal from him. In one institution several prisoners engaged me in a conversation, actually trying to avert my attention from a bag which I had left on top of a barrier in the prison library. The inmate standing closest to the bag, delicately and in an offhand manner, pushed it with his elbow. Another prisoner squatted in back of the counter in order to be able to search the bag quickly once it had fallen, and to take the more valuable items. At the same time, the first prisoner was supposed to apologize profusely and jump over the barrier and hand me the "untouched" bag.

One should try to avoid becoming a "sucker" who "allowed himself to be skinned." But if such an incident does occur, then one should forget about it so as not to be regarded as an informer who seeks help among the functionaries and brings repressions on the prisoners. A notification about the theft to the administration would have had a decidedly negative influence on further research.

Many apprehensions are connected with research conducted in men's institutions by women. These fears are rooted in the specific way of thinking about prisoners as sexually depraved criminals who, deprived of any hindrance, would readily commit rape. It would be difficult to contradict this completely, but one can notice that the prisoners control themselves and try not to reveal their emotions if the presence of a woman arouses sexual desire. In situations created by the administration, rape attempted in the course of the investigation would be quickly noticed and the possibility for the offender to find himself alone with his victim is nonexistent—it would be impossible to close from the inside the room in which the interview is conducted.

A female student, Z, held interviews with prisoners who were summoned one by one to the room; when she made it known that the interview had come to an end, the prisoner was escorted back to his cell. At one point, an inmate stood up, pulled down his trousers, and placed his penis on the table. The student, embarrassed by this unusual situation, managed to control herself, stood up, looked straight into the eyes of the young prisoner and quite calmly and in a surprised voice asked "Sonny, what do you want?" The mortified inmate quickly pulled up his pants and ran out of the room. A moment later Z called for the next prisoner, informing no one about the incident. No other disturbances of this sort occurred.

Some of the prisoners refuse to talk with women at all. It would be difficult to explain the reasons more precisely—some said that "they do not want to excite themselves unhealthily." The apparel of a woman interviewer is also very important. It should be inconspicuous but can be quite chic, a feature which the prisoners appreciate; they are more courteous and proud of the opportunity to talk "with an elegant woman." The reverse effect is accomplished if her clothes are frivolous or provocative while matching behavior is totally reprehensible. A woman dressed or behaving in such a way is usually regarded by the prisoners as a "whore." She evokes anger and aggression—the inmates either do not want to talk to her or are insolent and flirtatious and jeer: "Lady, why do you ask? Women should stay home and take care of children and not hang around jails."

Fear in the presence of prisoners is also undesired. Usually the inmates notice it quickly and ridicule such investigators, whether men or women. The prisoners claim that this attitude is the effect of viewing them as bandits who could attack their chosen victim at any moment.

A woman about 45 years old conducted a survey in a penal institution and was so afraid of remaining alone with an inmate that she demanded the presence of a member of the prison staff during one of the interviews. For this reason she was regarded by the functionaries as a "stupid bitch" and a nuisance, and by the prisoners as a "louse." To annoy her they admitted that they wrote down only "lots of rubbish."

Fear of the prisoners is also revealed in rigorous, attorney-like behavior. It upsets the prisoners and results in their perceiving such a person as "reptilian seed." Generally speaking, if none of these deviations occur, then the prisoners are more polite and inclined to cooperate with women, and there is no subject which they do not discuss openly. On the contrary, they talk about the most intimate problems more often and more willingly with female investigators.

4.

To Do the Study in
Any Way Possible

The Naive Incognito versus the Paranoid

The secret reality of a prison constitutes an unknown area about which it would be difficult to advance certain research hypotheses. I no longer speculate about what prison social relations may look like. Ideas accepted a priori are usually disastrous for a scientific study. This is why the scholar should not presume a rigid research procedure. By using various techniques, the investigator should strive toward a gradual limitation and greater precision of goals, and toward filling out and making more detailed the initial and general cognitive map. We can capture only such elements of human consciousness which in some way become elements of our inner experience. If this is the case, then for every scholar certain boundaries to understanding exist, delineated in part by the range of his or her experiences and social background.[1] This is particularly valid for the academic scholar who wants to understand the inmates and prison staff who constitute a community so very different from that of the investigator. Nonetheless, individual experience is to a certain extent constricted and determined by the position held in the given community. The scope of an individual's practical knowledge about social reality, even if the broadest possible, is always limited and constitutes only a small part of social complexities.[2]

In the prison community the differences of knowledge among individuals stem from their belonging to divergent social groups. For example, the "git people" isolate themselves from the "suckers" and the latter need not be familiar with the experiences of the former. The academic investigator, on the other hand, has the chance to discover differences in the knowledge and experiences of each of the groups or at least the essence of those differences. Quite possibly, the investigator can grasp them even better as an outsider, albeit one with a certain understanding.

As I have emphasized, I was unable to prejudge anything about the structure of the prison community; therefore, I decided to abandon the approach of an investigator of the verification type.[3] I did not opt for questions of the sort: "Is the institution divided into people, suckers, and fags?" If there are no such divisions (and this study will show that this is likely), then does that mean that there are no structures at all, or that some other type is present? Even if it were to become apparent that these divisions exist, then should we identify relations in that structure with those already known and described? The verification approach holds an inherent danger of imposing the way in which reality is viewed and, with the help of accepted criteria, sorting it by "forcing" its identification.[4]

The basis for studying an individual through his environment is the individual's opinions, which are not formulated with the intention of their eventual use by others for research purposes but are only an unhampered and direct confession.[5] The awareness of being examined can considerably alter the behavior of people. As I have already mentioned, this process can seriously distort the real picture of the prison community. The concealment of one's own research goals seems to be the best way for overcoming this obstacle.

It also appears to be necessary for another reason. Since it is impossible to determine precisely the scope and methods of research, there is no way to request permission from the prison authorities. Formally, after all, they could interpret the situation as "someone wants to conduct a study, but he doesn't know what or how." One could assume that a more or less clear-cut description of the aims of research would not provide the desired effects either. However, another path remains open. Groups of students from study circles have been admitted into penal institutions with questionnaires. This was allowed only if each group was accompanied by a faculty member. As sometimes the students were refused by the academic staff, I became their "salvation" and willingly accepted such a role. In this way I was able to visit the penal institutions and had occasion to meet my own scientific purposes. At other times I assumed the role of a survey worker (still as a student) and used this opportunity to penetrate prison reality. Thus, without drawing undue attention to my real intentions, I was able to carry out my research.

The investigations were conducted in conjunction with other research and with the help of standard techniques. The concentration of the attention of the prison community on the questionnaires made it possible to penetrate it and to accomplish my own purposes without drawing attention.

Investigators must remember that their very perception by the persons under examination is a form of contact with them. Control over that which is perceived is at the same time control over contact, and a limitation and regulation of that which is shown and transmitted is the limitation and regulation of that contact.[6] Those limitations will intensify, particularly in the case of totalitarian institutions, if the researcher is identified with some institutional form of social control and therefore when there is a conviction about the purposefulness of study and in perspective the disclosure of the recorded events.

For the inmates my official purpose of research became the object of a paranoid fixation while the contents of the answers to the questionnaire became the object of manipulation and control over that which is being revealed—this was their prey. Here lies the weak point of research conducted with the aid of standard techniques. The investigator who approaches research unconventionally and who sometimes takes into consideration the attributes of the subject—especially his attitude toward being examined—can turn those weaknesses into strengths.

In this type of institution, as well as others, the investigators are regarded as employees of other state institutions. As civil servants they are faced with the task of receiving information from the client, the person under examination. Just like civil servants they tell their clients to fill out a questionnaire or to answer questions posed during the interview. The activity of the investigator is concrete and definite, formally identical with that performed by officials in contacts with clients. After completing the research, the investigator becomes a private person, similar to a civil servant after work hours.

A certain mode of carrying out research seems to be the reason for defining science as a bureaucratic institution and the investigator as an official. The fact that the researcher can remain himself for twenty-four hours at a time is a rather loose representation which can be altered when it becomes sufficiently evident—sometimes to the displeasure of the interlocutors who often would have liked to meet him on a private footing. If in situations when the investigator should react and participate spontaneously, he remains concerned with documentation or analysis, then he will bring out aggression in others.

It is my contention that a decidedly better way of conducting research on the secrets of the prison is to do so in "private" time, while carrying out other studies. I often made it known to the respondents that I had undertaken the research on commission, for a wage, and that I was not personally interested in it. I was then able to observe the fate of my work. My lack of personal involvement could have been made part of my estimated attitude to the reality being examined.

The image that I presented to the prison community suggested to them that I could not use any research instruments other than the official ones. I made notes only when I was alone. But the construction of one's own research instrument (if only a plan of questions to be used in the interview) was not plausible and possible for yet another reason. The secret reality of the prison constitutes for researchers an unfamiliar terrain in which it would be difficult to formulate definite research hypotheses. Unacquainted with that reality, we do not know what to ask. Another hindrance in preparing an instrument is that one cannot ask direct questions such as: do you steal? Secret reality does not tolerate it. The only assumption I made about this reality is that it is secret. That and the closed circuit of information in the prison outlined my conduct. The absence of the instrument and the avoidance of making notes in the presence of the subject provided me with what concerned me the most: they enabled me to make my true research aims and hindered the subject's controlling the data I registered.

It seemed most correct to accept an open attitude. In order to do this, I had to pretend to lay aside the existing knowledge and adopt a *naive stand:*

• I am a tabula rasa, I know nothing about life in prison, and I do not know what I will find out, I reject all previous knowledge.

• I am a mirror, I gather all information with identical care, I neither select nor evaluate it from the point of view of its eventual significance. Here the basic principle is to retain a maximal faithfulness in relation to the described reality. There can be no bending of the actual social process to an assumed theory, nor the possibility of employing conceived research techniques.

• I am ignorant, and each of my interlocutors is a competent and equally valuable informer.

• I am a humble and patient pupil. If someone makes a statement concerning life in the penal institution, I have to wait patiently with pretended or authentic interest. I must take on the attitude of a pupil in relation to the narrator—he is the "professor" and I the good listener, modest and interested in the topic. I also used to ask for an explanation and, when necessary, repeated his thoughts in my own words, requesting confirmation that I had understood.

• I am amoral. I reject the possibility of evaluating deeds from the point of view of ethical criteria. I neither condemn nor praise that which I see and hear.

• I am a piggybank. I collect more or less secret information and offer none myself. I do not tell others what I have found out and from whom.

The acceptance of the cognitively naive stand generated certain directives for the behavior of the investigator in prison. They can be described most briefly as an unstructured way of spending time. Analogically stated, if one wants to familiarize oneself with the inner working of some machine, one should allow oneself to become part of it—to pass through all of its parts. No opportunity was too reprehensible for me not to learn the truth. If someone wanted to speak, I began a conversation. If someone wished to talk on a topic chosen by him, I discussed that subject. If a functionary invited me home, to a restaurant, or to go fishing, I accepted. If someone wanted my advice, I offered it. I did not define that which I wished to accomplish. The plan of my visit in the institution was a function of coincidences, chances, and opportune occasions. My behavior was submissive; others decided what I was to do, where I was to be taken, and what I talked about. I waited for proposals and made none myself, remaining a hunter who sought opportunities to make an acquaintance, to obtain some information or to scrutinize prison life.

From a certain moment, when a picture of the structure of the prison community emerged, my behavior became purposeful. I arranged meetings with certain persons in a discreet way. I stayed more often in chosen quarters or tried to establish rapport with people who interested me, because they were better sources of information or facilitated contacts with a larger number of people, or because I felt that for the general acceptance it would be better to seek the company of precisely those persons.

One has to assume that a certain period of time in prison and the collection of information contribute to losing naivete. There was a point when my attitude became dual: I behaved like a mirror, reflecting all information, but at the same time I turned my attention to those repetitive concurrences which create a picture of the relations within the prison community. On the basis of that knowledge I construed certain hypotheses and resultant questions, the answers to which would verify the correctness of my suppositions.

The Weak Aspects of the Secret

The characteristic feature of the secret is the fact that it conceals a certain state of affairs directed against someone or something. There is always an "addressee" or "addressees" (persons, institutions) from whom the secret keeper wishes that the information about the given state of affairs would be kept. For various reasons (official duties, threatened interests, suffered wrongs, the loss of good reputation) well known to those who share the secret, the "addressees" could react to the news in a way feared by the authors, and for this reason they keep the sources of their apprehension secret. They can divulge the secret only to those whom they trust, i.e., with whom they also share other secrets, and against whom they have a sanction. The prison community is well aware of such interaction mechanisms. It is also conscious of the fact that for someone to obtain information about an isolated group he must have a sanction against one of its members and, within the secret interaction imposed upon that person, obtain information about the remaining people. The awareness of this situation forms the basic premise for the emergence of prison paranoia. In the penal community special attention is concentrated on who contacts whom. Keeping track of contacts comes down to an estimation of whether those whom we know (with whom we keep company, with whom we share secrets) have contacts with people who could become undesirable addressees of our secrets—could prove to be harmful or lead us to harm. A functionary could jeopardize the prisoners, and therefore they keep track of the functionaries who contact the administration. Members of the privileged group in the prison community are careful of contacts between "their own" and members of other groups. A single functionary or prisoner will evaluate the contacts of his colleagues or friends from the same point of view. In such instances the intriguing thought always arises, "What did they talk about? What did he tell him?" Everyone's contacts are closely scrutinized to discover who keeps company with whom and to recognize the peril such eventual contact with another person invokes.

Inappropriate contacts can give rise to suspicion and seriously hamper life in prison for those who are unaware of the existence of such a basis for their evaluation. These contacts are simply avoided. This is why physical (or other) contact between members of the prison community makes it possible to notice and distinguish various groups.

What are investigators to do, or any other strangers, about the assumption that they are "unclean," i.e., that they can inform, and, willingly or not, harm others? If one keeps company with the prison staff, one is labeled "unclean" by the prisoners, and if one cohorts with the inmates, then one is regarded with suspicion by the administration who fear that the inmates "sell out the prison" and for whom the investigator becomes inconvenient. The best method is to talk with everyone. One must exploit every opportunity even if only to greet someone, to stop a passing person for a moment, to exchange a few words about the weather. It is best if such an encounter can be seen by others, but it should not be overheard. One has to act in this way with prison staff who hold different posts and ranks, are of various ages, and work in different places. The same holds true for prisoners who should be different ages, from various cells, pavilions, and places of work—in other words, with anyone who crosses our path. One should walk up and ask about anything at all: the whereabouts of the exit, the washroom, whether we are not disturbing them, and so on. Ignorant about the arrangements in the community, and by contacting everyone whom we encounter, we avoid an association with a certain category of members of the prison community which could prejudice others to see us as enemies. This makes it possible for our position as a blind person who does not know with whom he is really speaking, to be acknowledged as a normal state of affairs, and to assure that our contacts not become a source of surprise and speculations. The situation in which a stranger talks with everyone is recognized as quite normal.

This state of normalcy is a necessary condition for conducting research. Building on such a foundation by developing closer contacts with certain persons, but not forgoing certain tactical contacts, we safeguard the former from suspicions. Moreover, those who wish to establish rapport with us know that it isn't dangerous. Others merely register the contact itself. They shouldn't overhear conversations, and this holds true not only for the useful but also for the tactical contacts. The impression that contact with us is safe is intensified by a certain way of thinking on the part of the persons under examination in the situation of "universal contacts" created by us. The person who has tactical contacts can assume that those are the type of contacts we also maintain with others. The interlocutor who discloses details of prison life, on the other hand can suppose that this is what the contact with all the others consists of; as a result he feels safe, believing that everyone else does as well. Just in case, the whole community could accuse each other of secrets. The multiplicity of my contacts made it feasible to formulate such a charge against everyone. But let us remember that the basis for such an accusation is only contact with the investigator—one never strikes out with something which could be used to hit us.

Of course, it is not enough for persons under examination to talk with us on every subject without any apprehension. What follows is a brief discussion of what inclines inmates and functionaries to disclose secrets and the ways in which I induced them to do so.

The first contact with secrets. When gathering indelible impressions, it is important for the task to begin as early as possible, immediately after initiating field work. We cease to notice certain subtle traits or characteristics whose novelty was so striking, once they grow more familiar. Therefore, we are concerned with registering above all the reactions of the prison community to the very appearance of the investigator or the appearance and disappearance of certain persons in the social domain of the penitentiary.

When I found myself at a certain distance from a group of functionaries standing in the courtyard of the institution, I observed that they talked loudly and merrily, patting each other and moving around freely. As I approached so that I could distinguish what was being said, they grew quiet, stopped laughing, and moved less energetically than before. After I passed by, they resumed their previous behavior. I recognized that I was regarded as sufficiently alien to make it impossible for them to speak freely and on every topic in my presence—they had their own affairs. Similarly certain groups of the personnel preoccupied with themselves behaved this way toward their own colleagues. And there were those who caused no such changes in behavior.

While among the functionaries I noticed that the colleagues who approached them behaved unrestrainedly until they saw me. My presence embarrassed them. They became silent and then asked whether they were interrupting or whether they could come in for a moment because they had "something to discuss."

My curiosity was aroused by other situations as well—why, for example, did prisoners standing in the corridor make way for one functionary while others had to pass them as if they were on a slalom course? Why did the inmates walk up to certain functionaries and talk quite freely and move away at the very sight of another? Why, when I looked through the peephole into the cell, did the prisoner standing opposite the door who noticed that he was being observed say something to the other inmates out of sight at that moment (I found out later that he says: "Peephole" or "Attention, peephole"), while at other times no one watched the peephole?

Those and other similar situations made me aware of the existence in the prison of issues about which none of those present wanted me to hear. I also noticed that I was by no means an exception and that if one were to become sensitive to this sort of variegated and irregular "spatial" behavior, then one could see that it is quite considerable.

Past secrets enable the investigator to approach the secrets of the prison in general. With little effort much can be discovered about past events, already irrelevant in the sense that their disclosure causes no negative consequences for anyone (for example, the people involved have been released, have left the place of work, etc.). However, it should be remembered that there is always some conjecture that this event from the past could upset someone since it reflects discredit on the prison system as a whole.

Just as the absence from the prison of the person sanctioned reveals past events, so too can information be obtained about events which occurred in other penal institutions. Data of this sort are not dangerous for anyone, and although they may not have anything in common with the reality currently examined by the investigator, they reveal the world of the prison showing what takes place there and what is possible. Moreover, they train the imagination, make us sensitive to problems crucial for this particular community, restrict speculation about life in prison, and show what the community notices and finds particularly disturbing in related stories.

The relationship of the secret. The violation of norms which were devised to regulate coexistence in the prison community is guarded by sanctions. In order to apply a sanction for breaking a norm, someone must register the incompatibility of the behavior with the norms. Every community develops a certain system of vigilance comprised of formalized and non-formalized ways of detecting undesirable deeds and conduct. This system includes not only the organized institutions of the police, officers of investigation, detective agencies, and so on, but also daily observations made by members of the individual's social milieu. This informal system of vigilance which assumes various forms depending on the type of culture, customs, political system, religion, etc., is particularly effective for the regulation of behavior in daily contact, the settling of certain matters, professional work, and the like.[7] Its absence makes the application of sanctions impossible.

The nature of many social events is such that if not registered at the moment they occur then it is as if they never happened. We find out from the victim and the perpetrator that someone verbally insulted someone or slapped someone's face, assuming that the given blow left no traces on the victim's body. If the witnesses and participants share the secret, then the news about this event will never reach us.

We are dealing with a reality which is regulated by officially accepted norms. I have stated that behavior contrary to the norms is concealed—it is secret. But I have also noted that this type of behavior itself calls for regulation—and the latter is devised in prison. We are thus dealing with a new reality which is ruled by norms different from the "official" ones and which have been described as secret. There are, however, possible behaviors which break the principles of the secret world but which must also seek refuge in secrets. This third level of reality can, but does not have to, remain secret in relation to the first one. A certain relativity of secrets comes to the forefront.

If a prisoner had stolen an item from another prisoner, who is his colleague, then he infringed upon a norm which forbids theft both in the official and in the secret code—thieves can steal but not from each other. But if the inmate shakes hands with a functionary, something he is forbidden to do by the code of the prisoners, then the offender will try to keep this fact a secret. He does not have to do this in relation to other functionaries and can even calmly perform such an act before their eyes. Neither is shaking hands with a functionary kept secret from the investigator. By avoiding affiliation with both the prisoners and the prison staff—if possible—the investigator will quite easily find out about events which violate the norms of the outside world. In this way the investigator learns about the brutal treatment of the inmates by the staff from the prisoners themselves, and vice versa.

Disclosed secrets and enemy secrets. One can also discover the contents of disclosed secrets which the whole prison knows about. Relaying such information to the investigator is safe since the person involved can assume that everyone knows about the given event or fact and that the investigator could have found out about it from anyone. The inmates under examination also disclosed secrets of their enemies—individuals and groups—an act which could be used predominantly against those enemies.[8]

Unidentifiable secrets. Inmates talked about life in prison mainly in a general way, without giving detailed data identifying time, situations, and persons. They left many things unsaid and their stories were rather enigmatic. Later, having learned more about the penitentiary, it was possible to decipher their meaning.

The temptation of betrayal. Georg Simmel argued that a secret is accompanied by the temptation of betrayal similar to the pull of a precipice. It is true that many of the subjects succumbed to this temptation, usually in connection with a violation which they had committed or, as they admitted, with undiscovered "crooked deals." By keeping them to themselves the inmates were unable to revel in their own skillfulness, intelligence, courage, etc. They needed recognition, to make an impression, to boast; in an unrestricted conversation they were unable to refuse this temptation and, to use an expression taken from the inmates' vocabulary, they "told on themselves." But this wasn't the only motivation. Sometimes they were deeply dissatisfied with relations with fellow inmates or harbored resentment about wrongs suffered. The interview made it possible to relieve these pent up feelings.

"Losing one's head" in a conversation. Many of the interlocutors who had the opportunity to talk with an educated stranger rambled excessively and lost control over what they said, revealing events which I felt were secrets.[9] This was sometimes shown by their own reactions to the stories—having realized that too much had been said, they suddenly stopped and completely changed the subject or, claiming that they had made a mistake, corrected the narrative.

Illusory sanction. Since the initiation of secret interaction is possible only if one has, or thinks that one has, a sanction against one's partner, then, if that partner wishes to become part of the interaction, he should provide such a sanction against the other person. As a rule, people are unaware that having an effective sanction against another person is not at all that simple. Usually a sanction is identified with what is a sanction for ourselves. The disclosure of a violation committed by someone could in fact have negative effects, but the disclosure of the same act committed by another person does not necessarily have the same negative effect. This always depends on the specific situation of each of the persons. If, for example, the investigator curses, no one will do anything about it, but a prisoner in a similar situation risks at least a reprimand from the guard. The sanction is identified with something whose performance or disclosure is feared. Frequently, however, this fear is unnecessary—the disclosure proves not to produce any negative effects. These are the psychological traps into which we fall—sanctions in such cases are illusory. Nonetheless, if someone knows what it is that the other person fears, possession of a sanction can be assumed. In order to establish secret interactions with my interlocutors I provided them with sanctions against me. I drank vodka with the guards and "tea" with the prisoners. I brought the inmates tea, cigarettes, and food, traded with them, and passed correspondence. I admitted to crimes never committed and to my own immorality. This type of interaction, in fact, produced the best effects. Drinking vodka with the staff inside the penal institutions—the glasses were filled with a small portion of tea extract and pure vodka was added—and outside the prison was especially effective. Joint drunkenness brought us closer together. It was presumed that a drunken investigator shows his true self. It was on such occasions that I was asked what I "really came" for.

Loosening the tongues of the staff was different than that of the prisoners. In one respect, however, both communities were similar—they spoke more eagerly about others than about themselves.

I. The prison staff unwillingly described life in prison, and for this reason I spent more time observing their behavior, while the convicts provided much pertinent information. The technique of conducting interviews with the staff could be described as indirect provocation.[10]

1. The technique of demonstrating erroneous knowledge was used citing opinions of a fictional third person who was supposed to have uttered some totally false statement. For example, I said that I had met someone who claimed that he had sat in prison where the inmates performed the same work as the functionaries and even ate with them. This drew laughter or anger, and the functionary immediately responded: "That fool never sat in prison or if he did, they gave him so much crap he didn't want to admit it. Mister, here it's like this. . . ." "Faulty knowledge" gave rise to a wish to correct the false opinions and encouraged the functionary to speak so openly that he returned to the theme during the following meetings, still correcting the wrong opinion and providing me with much information.

2. The application of the technique of the conjectured thoughts and feelings of the persons under investigation was linked with a presumed critical evaluation by the staff of a certain state of affairs, their feeling of having suffered some wrong or being unappreciated, etc. In this case one should present a certain critical evaluation as one's point of view or point out the injustice experienced by the staff: "People think that you have nothing to do here. Lock up the prisoners in the cells and not much more. But I see hard work and aggravation." The reaction can be: "You're right. People don't know this and you too, after all, cannot see everything. There are such things here. . . ." Another possible approach is: "This warden seems to be acting so strangely toward me, that I'm afraid." The staff member retorts: "Not only toward you. Me and others too. You should see what he manages to do. . . ."

3. There is also the technique of expressing disbelief. If a staff member says something which could interest us, expressing his emotional involvement, then in order to continue or develop that trend we show our disbe-

lief: "We drank for about a week then." "Impossible, you must be boasting." "It's the truth, and that was nothing compared to a year ago when. . . ." Disbelief intensified in the interlocutor the need to convince us about the veracity of his story; as a rule he would cite numerous examples in order to confirm it.

4. An example of the technique of reticence is: if a functionary describes a secret (a breach of rules), then it is sometimes better to act as if nothing had made a great impression on us or interested us. One should simply listen as if the narrative concerned something normal or behave in a way which corresponds to the anticipated reaction. The wrong reaction in such a conversation results in changing the topic.

5. The technique of conformation is also used. If the subject of the interview is difficult (for example, if it concerns the immoral behavior of a member of the staff) and is connected with anxiety about our eventual reaction, then we need to meet him halfway and say something derogatory about ourselves. The purpose of this step is to make the narrator conscious of the fact that he is not speaking to a prude and that his words do not cause shock or disgust.

As a rule I used these techniques during the first stage of the interviews. My informant became accustomed to me and realized that he should not expect any repercussions. He simply became used to my presence. The degree of familiarity achieved later depended in part on the personality of the informants. It often happened that in making closer contact with a subject, it was subconsciously expected that I disclose some shortcoming of my own, or better, that I misbehave (e.g., drink vodka and get drunk).

II. The technique of holding a conversation with the prisoners can be described as sustaining. We begin with a neutral topic and at a certain stage notice that the prisoner is speaking. Showing interest in the conversation and accepting the prisoner is often sufficient to sustain the interview.

Prisoners are inclined to narrate events in an unstructured manner—they spin out associations.[11] Consequently at times we are simply flooded with a great number of stories told in a haphazard manner interlaced with unfamiliar abbreviations. It is difficult to concentrate the convict's attention on a single theme. When interrupted, the prisoners shy away and lose their train of thought and willingness to talk. It is much more politic to steer the conversation by showing increased attention during a description of some particularly interesting event, thus achieving a further expansion of that theme in the story. A similar effect is gained by nodding one's head at given points in the narrative. The absence of reaction or lack of interest curtails the statement and the inmate changes the subject.

A feature which is almost universal both in the thought and in the narrative of the inmates (and often of the prison staff) is thinking on the level of specifics. In the narrative this tendency is revealed in precise descriptions of activities performed or past events, often combined with an emotional attitude toward events and persons. Since these descriptions are rather picturesque they are easy to understand. The only problem is in understanding abbreviations or unfamiliar concepts.

Sources often feel protection in the often correct assumption that the investigator understands little of what is being said, which is usually the case at the beginning of the study. But with time and increased knowledge the situation totally changes. The investigator is capable of guessing many things and makes predictions and conjectures about them. At that point conversations intentionally held or overheard become increasingly meaningful and informative. But one should not correct the first impression of total ignorance regarding prison affairs which the investigator had made on his sources; it is much better to pretend to be deaf even if our hearing has returned.

In every conversation it is best to maintain a reticence. Excessive interest in prison matters should not be revealed. Although the time of the prison visit is usually restricted, one should not hurry—the knowledge must come naturally. What a subject says often prompts further questions in order to have everything explained to the very end. But this could be interpreted as suspicious curiosity and betray the investigator's considerable knowledge. At other times, disclosing one's knowledge and comprehension is very useful since it encourages the informant to further confession once he sees that he is understood and is not speaking to someone naive. Nonetheless, one should not demonstrate a great desire to know anything. This could give rise to wariness and paranoid fear of revealing something which could prove to be harmful. It is better to seem uninformed rather than guess more than the informant would wish. The attitude of being unsatisfied or being more or less suspicious about our interest in the inmates' "shady" deals gives the best results. By not flooding my sources with questions, I avoid revealing my own knowledge. In this way I put his suspicions at rest. This may even lead to some frustration that I am not sufficiently interested in his person and problems. This is just as well—one can't satisfy the subject with our interest in them without awakening suspicions about the purpose of the interviews. Through this an extremely important thing can be achieved: we leave the impression that the value of the information is not particularly relevant for us or in general. At the same time, we make the subject less suspicious.

"Breaking" the Prison Language

Wilhelm von Humboldt said that man lives only in such a world whose image is contained in language. My investigations basically dealt with secret prison reality to be found in prison language—the fundamental source of the data gathered was interviews. But one cannot describe human behavior in purely external terms—the social situation is created due to the meaning with which the actors endow their actions. This meaning is reflected above all in naming these actions and in a linguistic capturing of its principles. The intra-cultural way of interpreting phenomena is their essential feature and without taking into consideration the consciousness of the members of the group and their attitude toward their own activities and those of others (expressed linguistically), the phenomenon itself wouldn't be understandable.[12]

The process of becoming acquainted with the secrets of a prison community articulated in its language is connected with the necessity of a transmission into the investigator's language. This constitutes a framework for the explication of the vernacular of the prisoners. It is as if the same language and speech community were treated as "a field of action where the distribution of linguistic variants is a reflection of social fact."[13] The strange sound of the speech used by the persons under examination can, therefore, be the outcome of our ignorance about events which they know and describe. We are unable, even if we learn the vocabulary, to use it suitably for a given situation or in a context in which it could be aptly applied; in other words, we lack what is known as linguistic competence.[14] Gaining linguistic competence is possible only for those familiar with relations prevalent in a given community.

This unfamiliarity can be of another nature as well. Namely we are dealing "with a specific code which serves to conceal the ways that groups and individuals act, conscious of the fact that they are the object of exclusion and repression, and that their way of life remains in contradiction to the binding norms."[15]

The participants of undercover interactions can create a secret code, as a result both of the linguistic ambiguity of their activities and of the wish for safe communication.[16] The code can also become "a defensive measure in the cohesion of the group and at the same time a sign of closing up or the superiority of a given group in relation to others (. . .) The jargon is actually a counter-language of an ethnic community but also in the sense that its purpose is a conscious break with the universal nature of linguistic communication between people. Simultaneously, it is supposed to construct an intimate bond of communication within a certain group."[17]

The languages used by the inmates and the functionaries are decidedly different. The first, often described in literature on the subject as a "code" (*grypsera*), is full of unfamiliar expressions. Even those which sound familiar can have a meaning completely different for the inmates than for us. The strange sound of the speech of the prisoners can signify that its designates are just an unfamiliar state of affairs, by which I mean things not encountered in our daily lives. This is the case, for example, with the expression "paying out," which means to hit or touch a second person with the penis and which is a way inmates are degraded in the informal structure of their community. This strangeness does not necessarily mean that the investigator hasn't heard the designates—sometimes we are dealing with a different name for something that is well known to us: "to veq" means the same as to smoke cigarettes, "to grub" means to eat, and "screws" are functionaries of the prison staff. Many familiar expressions mean something quite different for the prisoners: "derby" for us is a type of a horse race while for the inmates it means group masturbation. "Horse" is one of the names for the penis, "hitting" or "whipping the horse" means masturbation, and a group masturbation to see who will reach orgasm first is known as a "derby."

The expressions created by the prisoners include all classes of relationships for which there are no detailed descriptions in our vocabulary: "red spiders" are party members as well as those who cooperate or maintain close contacts with communists, "reptiles" are functionaries of the militia and the prison staff, and "reptile seed" are those who intend to work in one of the two services. Special names are given to inmates who come from various parts of Poland. They not only indicate the place where they were born but a certain characteristic feature of criminals from those regions: "wise guys" come from Warsaw, "pen knives" from Łodz Rzeszow, "hobbyhorses" from Cracow, "Hans" from Silesia, "spuds" from Poznan, "kangaroos" from Szczecin, and "Knights of the Cross" from Olsztyn.

This description of some of the expressions and terms taken from the slang of the prisoners pertains to the relation between the sign and the object of its reference in extra-sign reality. So this is a semantic relation.[18] Linguistic signs can also be characterized from the point of view of their relation to the user—this relation is known as pragmatic.[19] The pragmatic relation expresses its interpreter (its certain states or properties) and in no case leads to the sign denoting its interpreter. But the pragmatic relation also creates the meaning of the sign. The latter is composed of both its relation toward the designated object and an inclination toward a definite reaction to that sign on the part of the persons using it.[20]

The pragmatic dimension of the meaning of the sign can be actually ascribed to each of the above mentioned prison expressions: "to pay out" means something negative, and the person using this sign knows that being "paid out" signifies humiliation and social degradation, while the "red spider" is a contemptuous expression, similar to "reptile" and "reptile seed."

Certain expressions used by the inmates have special pragmatic relevance. Saying them establishes important social facts. These signs are generally known as "curses" which, when addressed by one person to another contaminate the latter—degrade him and transfer him to the class of "suckers."[21] The "curses" include such terms as: cock, whore, lesbian, pretty, darling. A certain category of expression exists which annuls the effect of the "curses" and overrides the eventual outcome.

It seems that the pragmatic relation which expresses the attitude of the person using the sign as such supposes his knowledge both regarding the reference meaning of the sign and the social context of its application, its pragmatic meaning for others. It remains, therefore, connected with that which Kaymes calls linguistic competence. The way in which the user defines the situational context influences the choice of linguistic signs employed by him. The situation of speaking, therefore, is one of choice, which, in the case of the prison, is regulated by subculturally molded patterns.

The argot of the prisoners is a domain of exploration which is safer because it remains natural. I listened and encouraged the inmates to use it in conversation with me. The meanings of expression were explained using my own vocabulary which fulfilled the function of a meta-language, i.e., one in which sentences about a language are formulated—in this case about the speech of the inmate. This is how I attained my linguistic competence. The unfamiliar reality coded in it was possibly the greatest source of information about it.

The language devised by the functionaries did not constitute any kind of a distinct system. If a conversation with the staff dealt with any sort of a language then this was primarily that of the inmates. In this respect the personnel was more competent than I. Among the staff, I encountered the use of phrases borrowed from the prisoners—which they called the "prisoners' gabble"—as well as elements of the professional slang of the staff, but these occasions were few. In such instances I acted similarly as with the inmates and translated using my own vocabulary.

The Reconstruction of Social Reality of the Prison

Observed facts are always rooted in specific circumstances. Consequently, the first ascertainment of these facts is of an inferential nature—it is the result of selecting one of the many possible explanations of the given facts. The circumstances make it possible to recognize and create the meaning of that which occurred in the social exchange being observed.[22]

The first aspect of this logic says that the participants of the social exchange are perceived in categories which have a culturally prepared and disseminated meaning. Moreover, in the perceived situation there must be appearances which enable one to maintain those premises. The investigator must accept those premises despite the fact that the social context of the interaction is often unfamiliar and incomprehensible. Inferences made on the basis of the context of the interactions create, suitable for the given situation, a basis for predicting the future of the interaction and a general interpretation of what is happening. Principles deduced on this occasion are not isolated. When they are confronted with new experiences, it might prove necessary (or not) to prepare a new interpretation or later to recognize it as typical for isolated events. This reflection, or inference of principles, might signify the elimination or addition of information to the experiences stored in our memory, making it possible to formulate statements of a higher level of generality.

The following example illustrates this entire process.[23] A convict told me that some time ago a new inmate was assigned to his cell. Upon arrival, in front of everyone else, he touched his own sexual organs with both hands and then dipped his hands into a bowl of cottage cheese standing on a table by the door. He then stretched out his hands and, lightly shaking them, proceeded further into the cell, approaching each of the prisoners in turn.

At first it seemed to me that this could be a scene from an insane asylum—devoid of logic or sense. It proved to have been extremely sensible, and the behavior of the new inmate was rational, reflecting the rigid order ruling this community. The existence of this social context as well as of the fact that the action is understood by the persons being studied can be disclosed by a so-called reflective approach to isolated information simply by raising questions such as: "why?" and "what for?"[24]

Why did the prisoner act in the way he did? The response given by my source was this:

- the described inmate was a "git person" and wanted to belong to the "git people" in this particular penitentiary;
- "git people" form a privileged group;
- new prisoners are tested to see whether they are suitable to belong to the "git people";
- for example, they can be beaten and then the rest will see whether they inform the administration;
- information disqualifies every inmate;
- if new prisoners immediately show their anxiety, they can be labeled as "victims" through special ritual methods;
- one of the ways of "victimizing" is to touch a prisoner with sexual organs or touch something which came into contact with them;
- "the victims" are deprived of privileges, held in contempt by the "git people," and exploited by them;
- this particular person protected himself against eventual "victimization" or painful methods of testing him: by spilling the cottage cheese which came into direct contact with his sexual organs on his eventual aggressors, he could turn them into "victims";
- by approaching each of the inmates in the cell, the prisoner sensed who avoided contact with him—these were the "git people," while those who did not do so were the "victims";
- in this way the inmate identified the "victims" and discovered with whom he should not shake hands, an act that could "bring harm upon himself";
- the prisoner revealed familiarity with the principles of "hidden life" (social competence);
- he communicated that he is a "git person" and wishes to remain one (by his behavior he affirmed the existing informal structure).

From the description of this simple incident I found out about: the existence of informal divisions among the inmates; relations between distinct categories of the prisoners; ways of testing newcomers; ways of "victimization" and its avoidance; the prohibition of filing complaints to the administration.

The reconstruction of the prison social reality consisted precisely of the formation of a structure by using basic data. I accepted the universally expressed statements as true. I also treated as credible those statements which the other informants did not necessarily confirm in their "reflective preparation of isolated events" but which they did not negate. I accepted or rejected individual information pertaining to events either for reasons of discretion or because it was impossible to test them, depending on my estimation of their probability or occurrence. I estimated the veracity of those individual pieces of information on the basis of what I already knew about the community of the penal institution, and whose occurrence seemed to be likely in accordance with the specific rationality functioning in the given community. This is why the estimation of the truthfulness of certain information changed during the course of my stay in the institution.

The field work of the investigator does not consist merely of collecting data. Each cognitive act should constantly be accompanied by reflection on the very nature of the cognitive process[25] as well as by the continual intellectual examination of the material collected and its repeated confrontation with reality.

When I left the prison and did not have to meet any staff, I wrote down the events I had noticed and remembered, at the same time putting them into order. This was like trying to fit together fragments of a mirror dropped from a great height. The comparison of the data and the attempt to embody them into a whole often revealed gaps and imperfections in the findings which, in turn, led me toward further research.

It is impossible, of course, to gather all the fragments, but as their number grows and they are assembled into matching sections, a probable picture emerges of the whole—deformed and incomplete. But it grows less so from day to day, and at a certain stage it is possible to perform a general theoretical analysis.

The fragments collected in prison, the basis of which I reconstructed a picture of social reality, originated from diverse sources: data from observation, information taken from personal history files of the inmates, documents and studies made by the prison system, interviews with prisoners and staff, and items produced by the inmates.

Undoubtedly, the place where the picture of prison reality took shape was my imagination: it was more implanted in my head than in notes. I believe that I understand it much better than I am able to express it. After all, Cicourel argues that generally we are able to understand more in comparison with that which we can formulate according to normatively (grammatically) proper rules and suitable dictionary descriptions of objects and events.[26] This state of affairs is inherent in the very nature of cognition which consists of understanding based on empathy for someone else's experiences which are compared with our own. If one were to characterize the process of understanding according to Dilthey, then this is a certain ability to evoke in oneself a recreative experience, to put oneself in the situation of the subject, to accept and acknowledge the obviousness of his order of values.[27] The outcome of such research is always expressed in the investigator's particular subjective categories.

The Organizational-Technical Aspects of Investigations

Unfortunately, it was possible to make only a few on-the-spot notes from interviews and observations. Noting anything down in the presence of the inmates made them unwilling to continue talking and gave rise to fears that the notes could be used for something else. I never tried to take notes in front of the functionaries, and as a rule I prepared notes in my quarters in the evening, when I was no longer constrained by someone else's presence. The suspicions of the persons under examination and the anxiety not to act to their own detriment by talking with me were ever present and revealed whenever I tried to note down something or when I wanted to obtain more details about the subject. They unwillingly related personal information, and the interview usually ended in a fiasco. I therefore stopped trying to identify the subjects in that way. I recognized almost all of them by sight but rarely knew their names or anything at all about them. Even after starting to use the familiar "you," we addressed each other without knowing each other's Christian names. The majority of my informants were, therefore, anonymous sources of information which I would note down without associating it with its author.

I recognized those persons and talked to them in various places: at work and in school, in the cells, recreation hall, corridors, courtyard, outside the prison, in the homes of functionaries, in a restaurant, or while fishing.

These conversations lasted for a few minutes or several hours. I talked with persons whom I knew more closely for a few hours every day. Others I saw more rarely. There were also people with whom I conversed only once for a short period of time.

Sometimes the conversations were held with a large group of inmates or functionaries. Although I spoke with them I did not know them previously nor did I remember them later. But they, as a rule, remembered me, and then it seemed that strangers greeted me and talked with me as if I were their close acquaintance. The actual degree of close contacts with my informants thus varied. The contacts ranged from being told family secrets and asked, for example, to mediate in marriage problems or sharing the most intimate thoughts and problems (e.g., homosexual inclinations among the prisoners), to very superficial and formal ones. I tried to make these contacts as varied as possible—I talked with prison functionaries of different ranks and duties, from all age groups, and with inmates of different ages, employment, quarters, and position in the informal structure.

The prisoners whom I contacted were predominantly selected at random for parallel research with the aid of a questionnaire, and those who held different ancillary functions in the prison administration and to whom access was easiest. As for the functionaries, my contacts were primarily those responsible for the organization and course of my investigations, i.e., mainly the counselors and guards. Through them I became acquainted with the remaining functionaries and employees of other departments of the prison staff.

As a result of the way I worked in the penal institutions I was unable to calculate precisely the number of people with whom I talked. In institution A I met about 300 prisoners—30 percent of the total number of inmates, and 40 functionaries. In B I talked with about 200 prisoners—14 percent of the population—and about 25 functionaries, and in C—with 80 prisoners—that is 9 percent of the total number—and 25 functionaries.

I usually spent from six to ten hours daily in the given prison and met its staff members outside the institution. Whenever there was an opportunity I collected and photographed various objects connected with prison life: items made by the prisoners, drawings, and souvenirs. Many of them I either purchased from the inmates or received as gifts because, for example, they were confiscated during a search and were to be destroyed. I was greatly assisted in this task by the students. I was also able to use a study dealing with the informal structure of the inmate community prepared by the functionaries from the institution. Finally, I became acquainted with other documents, mainly with the personal history folders of the convicts.

I spent six weeks in institution A: four weeks at the end of January and the beginning of February 1975, and two weeks in May 1977. In institution B I worked for four weeks altogether: two weeks in July 1977, and two weeks in July 1978. In August and September 1980, I stayed for two weeks in institution C. In the course of my research, I lived in the guest rooms belonging to all three prisons.

5.
Prisons Selected for the Study

Gaps in Previous Research

In Part 2 I will deal with those social events in correctional institutions which were not disclosed by their perpetrators since, as a rule, they are violations of the officially accepted rules of social coexistence. The perpetrators themselves create sui generis rules regulating the life of the inmates as well as the social forces responsible for their observance. It is exactly this world of secret social events, together with their specific regulations, which in literature is known as the "hidden life" of penal institutions.

This "hidden life" includes three stages of interpersonal relationships: among employees of the prison administration, among the prisoners, and between the administration and the inmates. Polish research has concentrated chiefly on relations within the community of the prisoners and only to a slight degree on the attitudes of the inmates toward the administration. Not much is known about the attitude of the administration toward the prisoners and virtually nothing on the subject of relations within the administration itself. A description of all three groups of relations, made on the basis of investigations conducted in three penal institutions is included in Part 2, "Behind the Facade of Formal Organization."

Most of the few existing studies into "hidden life" were carried out in institutions for juvenile delinquents and reformatories for children and youth,[1] and less so in prisons, and even then primarily in prisons for juveniles.[2] Research in penal institutions for recidivists is very rare (one study for each institution).[3] Each of these investigations, however, is deficient from the point of view of the subject at hand. In this situation, the formulation of any sort of statement or generalization carries a considerable risk of error.[4] Furthermore, there are no works whatsoever dealing with semi-open penal institutions.

Varieties and Types of Penal Institutions

The Executive Penal Code divides penal institutions into: work centers, ordinary penal institutions, transitory penal institutions, penal institutions for juveniles, penal institutions for recidivists, and penal institutions for convicts requiring special medical measures.[5]

The basis for distinguishing these varieties of penal institutions admitting felons sentenced to imprisonment were various factors such as: age, the nature of the crime, previous record, degree of social deviation, and progress in resocialization (as in the case of the transitory penal institutions to which a convict can be sent after earlier confinement in other types of institutions).[6] Furthermore, the penal institutions can be divided into types,[7] and the foundation of this typology is the regime of the confinement, together with the functional architecture, the categories of the convicts, and the principles of suitable penitentiary policy. These types include: (1) a closed penal institution (the convicts stay the entire time within the bounds of the institution); (2) a semi-open penal institution (the convicts work outside the institution to which they return after work); (3) an open penal institution (in reality non-existent).

My research deals with those examples which reflect the differentiation of the organization of penal institutions. The differentiation was conducted mainly from the point of view of:

1. the degree of isolation of the inmates from the outside world and the resultant prison regime defined by the type of the institution: closed penal institution; semi-open penal institution.

2. age and previous confinement in penal institutions (prison experience) expressed in the varieties of institutions: penal institutions for juveniles (17-21 years of age); penal institutions for first offenders (21 years of age and over); penal institutions for recidivists (multiple offenders).

I have omitted other institutions because of their small number or atypical character (for example, those intended for the mentally ill).

A Prison for Juveniles (Institution A)

In this institution sentences are served by people from 17 to 21 years of age. There are also inmates older than 21. This is permitted by ruling no. 11 issued by the Minister of Justice on January 25, 1947, regarding the existing regulations for confinement in which paragraph 19 of decree 2 says: "Convicts who are over 21 years of age can continue to serve their sentences in penal institutions for juveniles if this is purposeful for reasons of resocialization or because of the short period of time left until release." This decision is supplemented by paragraph 20 which says that convicts older than 21 years of age can remain in an institution for juveniles "if this is supported by reasons of resocialization and especially by the need for a didactic influence of the environment.'' The number of these convicts in penal institutions for juveniles is determined by ruling no. 1 issued by the Central Director of the Penitentiary Administration (January 10, 1975) in which paragraph 22 says that: ''Adult convicts can serve sentences in penal institutions for juveniles and all told number of the adult convicts, mentioned in paragraph 20 of the regulations concerning confinement cannot exceed 25 percent of the population of the penal institution for juveniles.''

In 1976 and 1977 there were about 1,000 convicts in institution A who served sentences in a rigid and basic regime. Juveniles who had no more than ten years left to serve and who belonged to health categories A, B and C were also conveyed here.

The institution includes a carpentry shop employing the majority of the convicts. They make crates, wooden containers, chairs, and wardrobes. The inmates perform simple tasks and, although machines and tools are used, most of the work calls for physical strength and average manual skills—making crates, gluing, handling carpentry machines. The prisoners also clean up, transport raw materials and products, unload and arrange timber in a sawmill belonging to the factory, and so forth. Persons employed in the production of particular articles are judged according to imposed norms which estimate the number of items to be made. The administration of the factory includes civil workers (not members of the prison staff). The management, foremen, and other workers in the factory deal with the organization and overseeing of production, while the prison staff are responsible for controlling the behavior of the inmates.

Penal institution A also has auxiliary shops. According to the official classifications of the Central Administration of Penal Institutions the work performed in this factory includes small-scale metal and wood production, book binding, electrical equipment and radio-television mechanics. Actually, this comes down to small jobs in the workshops which are part of the training provided by the elementary vocational school (and vocational high school). The school has few tools and machines, and large-scale production is not possible. The school workshops offer more extensive service only to the penal institution. The primary school in A is attended by all inmates with incomplete elementary education.

The convicts are employed as assistants in the prison administrative offices, the laundry, the kitchen, and the boiler room. They perform various chores as orderlies, in the library, the barbershop, the recreation hall, and the radio network, and they make posters and bulletin boards.

A Prison for Recidivists (Institution B)

In 1977 and 1978 institution B had about 1,500 convicts sentenced mainly on the basis of article 60 paragraph 2 of the criminal code. These are therefore people previously convicted by the courts on at least two occasions for committing the same or similar crimes. The majority are adults, although there are so-called juvenile multiple offenders as well.

Institution B has a metal shop employing most of the convicts, making chain-link fences, containers, and other metal articles. It also has a large machine park with lathes, milling machines, galvanization tubs, presses, and other equipment and tools necessary for production. The prisoners working here are expected to have special skills. This is why, apart from training its own specialists needed by the factory, the institution admits recidivists with appropriate qualifications from other penitentiaries. Prisoners employed in the factory are accounted for according to the imposed norms of production. The metal shop is administered by civil employees, but prison staff oversee the inmates' behavior.

Institution B also has auxiliary workshops where cardboard boxes are made and books bound. As part of an assembly system of production the prisoners work on electronic equipment.

Just as in institution A, the inmates are employed in administrative and janitorial work. There is a primary school which has "periodic" vocational training courses, mainly for those jobs required by the prison enterprises.

A Semi-open Prison for First Offenders (Institution C)

In institution C terms are served by adults over the age of 21. The majority have already served part of their sentences in closed penal institutions and were transferred to institution C for the final part of their terms (usually from three to five years). The inmates are classified as suitable for confinement in a semi-open institution (imprisonment for petty crimes, good behavior). They are subject to a basic or lenient regime, and hold health categories A, B, and C.

In 1980 there were about 900 prisoners in institution C. Almost 90 percent worked in state enterprises outside the prison in nearby villages and localities. Select groups were transported to work in brickworks, sawmills, furniture factories, bus factories, and state agricultural farms.

The institution has so-called external departments which are somewhat like branches of the penitentiary located next to state agricultural farms (some managed by the institution itself). For this reason, institution C primarily admits inmates with a farming background. The convicts are periodically employed in building roads, flood campaigns, forestry, etc. In the institution itself a small group of inmates makes rubber articles. Some prisoners, as in institutions A and B, are assigned to administrative work or cleaning. The inmates employed by these enterprises are subordinated to the administration of the enterprises in fulfilling production tasks. Their behavior is constantly or periodically controlled by the prison staff (the patrol system). The latter also monitor the transportation of the inmates to their workplaces and back to the prison. The convicts can supplement their education in a vocational high school and an elementary school, both situated in the institution.

The employment of prisoners in institution C is dictated by imposed economic plans, not according to the production value, but the number of work hours. Hence the institution has made agreements with certain branches of the state economy which suffer from shortages of workers, and hires out its work force. There is a regional shortage of workers in the area in which the institution is located, and, in practice, many enterprises make efforts to employ the prisoners. In this situation the position of the institution, or more precisely of its directors, remains strong in the region.

PART TWO

Behind the Facade of Formal Organization

6.

Among "Crooks"

"People" and "Suckers": A Dichotomic Model of "Hidden Life"

The outcome of the existing research into "hidden life" seems to suggest that we are dealing with the same form in all prison institutions. It is true that investigations indicate certain transformation within "hidden life," both in time and space, but the basic elements and functions of that structure appear to be constant.[1]

A constitutive element of "hidden life" is the informal structure of the community of the prisoners. The inmates are divided among themselves into "people" and "suckers." An unwritten code, a system of norms and principles, places the "people" in a privileged position and deprives the "suckers" of all rights.[2] Some investigators point to the existence of a stratification among the "people" and the "suckers" but this does not alter the fact that the former enjoy privileges and the latter are deprived of them and remain the subordinates of the "people."

The "people" constitute an organized group headed by a single or several leaders. Their behavior is regulated by the norms and principles which bind the members of the group and govern three spheres of relations.

1. The relations between the "people":

• the "people" are equal, a "person" cannot exploit another "person," steal from him, or force him to do something; a "person" cannot serve another "person," for example, launder his underwear or socks;

• a "person" is not allowed to inform the administration on another "person";

• the "people" are forbidden to perform homosexual acts with each other;

• conflicts between the "people" are solved according to established rules;

• a "person" is ritually expelled from a group for breaking the norms.

2. The attitude of the "people" to the "suckers":

• the "people" are not permitted to enter into any sort of a partnership with the "suckers" (cannot shake hands, eat meals at the same table, maintain social contacts);

• all forms of violence and exploitation of the "suckers" is permissible (beating, rape, the taking or stealing of money and other items, forcing to work, etc.);

• a "sucker" essentially cannot become a "person."

3. The attitude of the "people" to the administration:

• no partnership contacts with employees of the administration are allowed;

• it is not permitted to work with or work for the administration (unpaid work, informing, etc.);

• one can refuse to work, to carry out orders, etc.;

• the "people" are united in the face of a threat on the part of the administration.

The "suckers" are not a group but constitute a certain social category. The "people" decide who belongs to this category and to a certain measure steer the life of the "suckers."

This model of an informal structure of the prison community, universal in Polish resocialization centers, is of a distinctly dichotomic character.[3] A certain similarity between "hidden life" in Polish and American correctional institutions is even perceived.[4] Aside from the problem of the similarity of the informal structure of the prison communities in American and Polish penitentiaries, however, it is not at all certain whether this model is retainable for Polish prisons.

In this chapter I propose a model of an informal structure within the community of the inmates of institution A, which negates the universal character of the dichotomic model. I also demonstrate that a feature which can be described as the unwritten prison code is not universally present in prisons and does not have to regulate the behavior of the inmates. Although it exists in institution A, in institution B the conduct of the inmates seems to be steered by an illegal market and not by any sort of an unwritten code. I also present yet another model of a "hidden life" which, together with the two previously outlined ones, should convince us that its representation ultimately depends always more on the concrete conditions prevalent in the institution than, for example, on the age or prison experience of the convicts.

*"Git People," "Fests" and Others versus
the Dichotomic Model of "Hidden Life"*

The juvenile offenders of institution A made their first direct contact with "hidden life" while under detention (with the exception of the former inmates of correctional institutions and reformatories). Here they were informed about the division into "people" and "suckers" in the prison. If during the period of detention they learned the vocabulary and principles of the "code" then they were admitted as "people."

It is rare for prisoners whose position in the structure of the prison community was not previously determined to be directed to institution A. For example, inmates described in detention as "suckers," in A already belong to the "victims." But the structure of the inmate community in A is not dichotomic, although one can distinguish in it certain clearly delineated social categories: fests (trusties); git people; the Swiss; victims; fags.

"Git people"

Members of this group call themselves the "code users." The "people" regard the social system in People's Poland as faulty. Law, in their opinion, is too strict and unjust. They claim that if it were possible they would serve other states and endeavor to undermine the existing system in Poland. They make plans for sabotage or attempted assassinations. The "people" maintain that after their release they will either work dishonestly or not at all. They do not intend to break off contacts made in prison; on the contrary, they hope to retain them and jointly realize their plans. The first thing the "git people" do after discharge is to settle accounts dating from their stay in prison.

The "people" do not consider a woman to be a person. "They all betray, denounce, are always ready to sell themselves, and are mentally and physically weaker." The "people" believe that prison is the worst place on earth but that a person who survives all of its hardships becomes experienced, hard, and knowledgeable. "No honest person will come to work in prison." The prison staff is the enemy, and they are not seen as human but simply as "screws." A sentence should be served in such a way as to contribute as little as possible to the intervention of the "screws into our affairs." The "people" have contempt for the possibility of rewards and distinctions. They believe that the inmates are divided into "people" and all the rest, known as "victims" (including the "fests").

Members of the group are obliged to:

• maintain the superiority of their group over others. The newly accepted member of the group is taught to treat the "rest" from "above" as something worse;

• respect personal dignity and that of the remaining members of the group. One is not allowed to treat the other members as inferior, and everyone has the same rights;

• maintain solidarity even after discharge. One cannot merely stand by while another member of the group is being assaulted by some other group; he must be helped. A member of the group is to be protected by all possible means from "wrong" suffered at the hands of the administration. A "git person" beaten by a "screw" in a prison corridor cried out, "People, save me," and the "people" responded by banging against the doors of the cells with benches and shouting for the beating to cease;

• provide mutual material aid—offering cigarettes to inmates locked up in solitary confinement as punishment, sharing food;

• be subordinate to those members who hold higher places in the hierarchy of power and decide about all the affairs of the group;

• sanction the principles accepted by the group. A violation of those principles is penalized by expulsion from the group;

• approve of behavior which hinders the work of the administration, e.g., the refusal to work or study, self-inflicted injuries, bad behavior toward the staff.

"Fests"

The majority of these persons plan to "arrange things" for themselves in such a way as to live comfortably, work, and earn well. They do not want to make any new or retain old acquaintances with people from the "criminal world." "I don't want to go back to prison and I don't need acquaintances from there." "The most important thing is to have work, a wife and a home and you can shove the rest . . ." "There's no reason to complain about my lot, if I weren't so stupid I wouldn't have gotten caught or done that in the first place." Confinement should be survived as comfortably and quietly as possible. No trouble-making and one can cooperate with the administration since it makes survival easier, but one must not go too far. The convicts must help each other. Those who make "survival" difficult must be expelled from the group and combated.

Members of the group are obliged to:

• treat their group as the only suitable one. Its lifestyle makes survival possible;

• respect one's own dignity and not interfere in the interests of the other members of the group; it is permitted to have "deals" of one's own and one should not impede other members (this is profitable for the whole group);

• observe solidarity. When a "fest" is unfairly threatened by a member of another group or a functionary, he must be protected;

• sanction the principles accepted by the group. The breaking of these principles means exclusion from the group without a chance for readmittance;

• remember that unpaid work for the institution is acceptable. One can hold various functions (an orderly, recreation hall attendant, barber, etc.), since "it is easier to endure by good cooperation with the administration."

Norms binding for the "people" and the "fests" include the following:

• It is forbidden to shake hands with members of another group.

• It is forbidden to steal objects belonging to members of one's own group.

• One should not lie to members of one's own group if the matter is serious.

• It is forbidden to play the passive (female) role in homosexual intercourse.

• It is forbidden to launder someone else's socks, underwear, shorts, and other personal garments (with the exception of those working in the laundry).

• It is forbidden to "curse" members of one's own group (unless one wants to exclude someone from the group).

• It is forbidden to eat while someone else is using the toilet or with an open toilet nearby.

• It is forbidden to pick up objects which fell into or near the toilet.

• It is forbidden to put "unclean" objects on the table since the table might become "contaminated."

• It is forbidden to lift or carry items belonging to unknown persons (cigarettes, mugs, etc.).

• It is forbidden to shake hands with a member of one's own group early in the morning, before washing and using the toilet.

• It is forbidden to wash the toilet bowl with a cloth and even more so with bare hands; only a stick or another implement may be used.

• It is forbidden to eat meals served by a "victim."

• It is forbidden to take a lit cigarette offered by a member of another group.

• It is forbidden to handle personal articles (knife, spoon, mug) belonging to members of the same or another group.

• It is forbidden to eat at the same table with "victims"—the latter are not allowed to sit down at the table.

• One cannot complain to or inform about a member of one's own group to the administration.

The structure of power is identical for the "fests" and the "git people." The highest authority is the gathering of the leaders of cell blocks who in turn select the head of the whole penal institution. He is the direct superior

---

The Structure of Power in the Groups of the "Fests" and the "Git People"

Norms valid only for the "people"	Norms valid only for the "fests"
It is forbidden to handle keys (the "screws" carry keys).	It is permissible to handle keys.
A victim can be accepted into the group, but only after he performs certain tasks, whereas a "fest" can be accepted immediately as long as he did not belong to the "fests" for more than two years.	"Victims" cannot be accepted into the group, but "people" are accepted.
It is forbidden to use "fest" terms: "eat" and "fest," for example.	It is forbidden to use "people" terms: "grub" and "git," for example.
It is permissible to file complaints of assault to court.	It is forbidden to file complaints of assault to court.
	It is forbidden to tattoo oneself before the end of a year (the time to reflect on one's own status).

---

of the leaders of cell blocks and they, in turn, of the leaders of cells. Not every cell has its leader, and this depends on the number of members of a given group in the cell and on the trust or position of the convicts in that cell.

The leaders of cell blocks, led by the head elected by them, decide on the most important matters: the alteration, introduction, alleviation, or intensification of certain principles; moves as regards other groups; the change of the leaders of the cell blocks; the acceptance of new customs which emerged spontaneously; the resolution of controversies not settled at the cell block level.

It is impossible to hold meetings of the leaders of cell blocks since they live in different cells and cell blocks. Additional difficulties are caused by the control of the administration and the security system. This is why in instances mentioned above the leaders of the cell blocks inform the head of the institution of their stand (on various occasions) and, on the basis of their opinions, he makes decisions which are passed on to them. For less important issues, as well as for those that call for quick decisions, the head of the institution does not consult the leaders of the cell blocks.

Upon leaving the penal institution, the head proposes a successor from one of the eligible members of the prisoner elite. If the candidate agrees, then he becomes the new head of the penitentiary. The transference of power takes place in the presence of the elite, which notifies the more important members of the group about the choice of a new leader. This procedure does not concern the insignificant members, since they are uncertain, timid and, if pressed by the administration, could reveal the identity of the new head.

In each cell block the "git people" and the "fests" have their leaders who settle all affairs concerning the given group. They are assisted by three or four convicts (potential successors) who fulfill their functions during the leaders' absence. The leaders also include those inmates who were appointed to that post by those members of the groups who were temporarily assigned to places of work or study. It is their duty to contact the leaders and carry out their orders. The leader and the elite also decide about such matters as: membership of persons of uncertain status; the expulsion of a member; ways of solving controversies in the group; the issuing of sentences and administering punishment.

The leaders and the elite exercise power through the intermediary of assigned executor appointed from among members of the group in work and school, and in the cells. This style of functioning enables the head of the institution and the elite not to risk repressions on the part of the functionaries and to conceal their activity. The majority of the members of the elite belong to inmates known for their good conduct. The executors of the orders issued by the head have their own assigned and permanently fulfilled functions. They can be divided into executors who are either: (1) appointed to carry out orders concerning the external issues of the group; or (2) appointed to settle controversial problems with other groups (for example, the task of provoking the "git people" to begin a fight: the "fest" chosen for this task has physical prowess, never strikes first and, once hit, always wins; if the fight is noticed by the administration and its participants are penalized then he always appears to have been the one who was provoked by a blow and as a result is less severely punished).

Leaders also sometimes appear among the "victims." Their authority is founded mainly on physical strength and is exercised only over a part of the group. Not everyone heeds their orders and sometimes members even do the reverse.

The "fests" and the "git people" have a greater impact on the "victims" than the usually short-lived leader. Sympathy for one of those groups divides the community of the "victims." The group which treats the "victims" better enjoys the support of the majority.

"Victims"

The "fests" and the "git people" regard the remaining convicts as "victims."[5] The way in which someone was "victimized" expresses the degree of contempt, humiliation, or disdain and depends upon the type of norm or norms which the prisoner violated by his behavior. "Victimization" includes:

- "cursing": typical obscene and abusive curses are: cock, whore, lesbian, prostitute, masturbator, oaf, thug, drop on your cock, fuck your ass, fuck off, etc.; a "curse" said to a member of one's own group turns him into a "victim" but one addressed to a member of another group does not degrade him;
- "turning into a fag with a scepter": sprinkling with the brush used for cleaning toilets;
- "mucking": striking with a cloth dipped in the toilet bowl;
- "throwing down the toilet": forcing the hand of the person who is being degraded into the urinal or toilet bowl;

• "paying out": touching or striking with a penis an uncovered part of the body, most often the face, of the victim;
• homosexual rape.

Prisoners who were "cursed," "mucked," "thrown down the toilet," or "turned into fags with a scepter" are known as "victims." The "victims" do not observe any rules. Neither do they pay attention to their own language: "I say what I want and how I want to, no one pays any attention to me, I'm left in peace."

"The Swiss"

Those prisoners who have left the "fests" or the "git people," or who do not wish to belong to a group, and who have not been "victimized" in any way, are known as the "Swiss." They declare their neutrality and non-involvement in "hidden life." This category of convicts includes all those who were "victimized" but who, as a result of their persistence and efforts to be treated as the "Swiss," are considered as such. The group is composed above all of older inmates. They are included by the "fests" and the "git people" into a better category of "victims." It is forbidden to harass them, and the "fests" can even sit at the same table with them. The main motto of the "Swiss" is to quietly serve their terms. They do not observe any rules with the exception of not sharing a table with the "victims" and "fags." The "Swiss" have no leader and remain an unorganized group.

"Fags"

Prisoners who have "been paid out" or were raped are labeled with the derogatory term of "fags." The majority seem to be mentally deficient, passive, dependent upon others whose orders they carry out. Some are homosexuals who receive gratuities for their services (e.g., cigarettes).

The principles of transition from one group to another

The "fests" do not accept "victims" into their group. Once someone becomes a "victim" he is unable to return to the "fests." The "people" permit readmittance, which is by no means rare. Not every "victim," however, can be accepted by the "git people." These include prisoners "victimized" for their cooperation with the administration and "typical fags."

Granting the rights of a "git person" to a "victim" is known as "raising to the rank of a person." In order to become a "person" again one has to perform one or more tasks set by the leader of the cell block and his assistants:

• supply a given sum of money or its equivalent in food or alcohol. The size of the sum depends on the way in which the "victim" was "victimized" and on his subsequent position in the group. The lowest sum is 500 złoty, but as a rule it amounts to 1,000 or 2,000 złoty, or even more;

• "muck" a member of the "fests";

• force another convict to prostitute himself;

• perform an act of self-mutilation;

• conduct a long-term refusal to work;

• attempt escape from prison.

After scrutinizing the "prison biography" of the "victim" and the performance of the assigned task, the leader of the ward decides whether to "raise him to the rank of a person" or leave him among the "victims." In the case of a favorable decision, the leader and his assistants shake hands with the former "victim," thus turning him into a "code user," and drink symbolic "tea."

A "fest" who wants to become one of the "git people" (and who was not "cursed" for leaving the "fests") is not obliged to fulfill any of the above mentioned tasks. If he was a member of the "fests" for longer than two years, enjoys suitable support, and is vouched for by "significant" members of the "git people," then the leaders immediately decide to admit him. Similarly, a "git person" is admitted to the "fests" without the need for any additional conditions, as long, of course, as the "gits" did not "curse him" earlier for abandoning their group.

Norms regulating conduct toward the "victims"

The following principles are binding for the "fests," "git people," and the "Swiss":

• not to sit down to a meal together with the "victims";

• not to shake hands with a "victim";

• separate storage for dishes and toilet articles;

• a "victim" cannot sleep in a bunk bed above a "git person" or a "fest";

- meals served by a "victim" are refused;
- it is forbidden to sit on a school bench on the right hand side of a "victim" (this is traditionally the place of a woman);
- it is permitted to accept an offered cigarette (the "git people" can take it from a pack and the "fests" directly from the hand of a "victim");
- it is permitted to sit down at one table with a "victim" in the recreation hall to play chess, dominoes, checkers, etc. If the game is held in a cell, then a blanket must cover the table in order to prevent it from being "contaminated";
- one can borrow books, notebooks, writing utensils and newspapers from the "victim."

Countrymen and tea drinkers

The convicts label prisoners who come from the same regions as "countrymen." The "countrymen" help and support each other in difficult situations but only within the same social category. A "git person" (or a "fest") and a "victim" from the same part of the country do not maintain contacts (even if outside the prison they were brothers or neighbors).

The cells also contain groups composed of two, three, or four persons, whose members share cigarettes, tea, food, problems, etc. They are known as "tea rooms" or "wafflerooms" and acquaintances from such a group are called "waffles" or "tea drinkers." A few years ago a "tea drinker" meant an inmate with whom one drank tea, and a "waffle" an inmate with whom one shared everything (a close person, someone with whom one could share the Christmas wafer). Tea is prepared and drunk by the prisoners in secret. The inmates actually drink an infusion so strong that there have been cases of death brought about by its long-term consumption. Tea is the most sought after article. The prisoners take tea only within particular social categories.

Relations between groups

The "fests" claim that the "git people" are inconsistent in adhering to the principles which they often break and change at their convenience. They also regard themselves as the true keepers of the principles, who "do not permit any concessions." In contrast to the "git people," the "fests" do not accept "victims" into their groups and do not file complaints to the courts about assault. The "fests" and the "git people" use a similar language. Both admit that with the exception of a few words, their speech is identical. The "fests," however, maintain that they differ from the "git people" in the purpose of their language: "The git people use the code for the administration but we do it for ourselves." They are also indignant at the fact that the "git people" call eating, a basic human activity, "grubbing." "Only animals grub and people eat." "We say that we eat and they grub"; for this reason the "fests" call them "grubbers who act like animals." They fight among each other and beat up members of other groups, as a rule weaker ones. The "git people" are also condemned by the "fests" for planning future crimes and causing trouble in prison.

The "git people" regard the "fests" as "victims" and accuse them of cooperation with the administration, with informing, handling keys, and committing "wrongs" in relation to the "people." They promise to take revenge upon the "fests" after release from prison. The "git people" maintain that the "fests" are weaker and more cowardly and that many of them, after admittance to the "git people" or being discharged, add to their tattooed ladybird (which is the symbol of the "fests") a bayonet piercing it and the words "Death to the Fests."

The "fests" and the "git people" can share a table. If the "fests" outnumber the "git people" they can forbid them to sit down. The reverse situation usually does not occur—the "git people" are afraid of intervention by the prison staff.

The "fests" oppose the "git people" in a program-like manner. They are unable to use force for this purpose (the "git people" could file a complaint to court and the administration also could punish them for assault), and therefore use other methods such as "placing mines": a "fest" might steal cigarettes belonging to a "git person" and put them under the bedding of another "git person." The "victim," looking for his property, finds the cigarettes under the mattress of a member of his own group and informs the other "people" who might expel the accused. Another way is for the "fests" to inform the "git people" directly that one of their members "squealed" or committed a misdeed (and was seen by the "fests"); he also could be alienated from the group. Sometimes, the "fests" prepare secret notes whose author, supposedly a "git person," informs a significant member of the "code users" about the culpable behavior of another "git person."[6] As a result, the accused could be rejected by the group. The "fests" seem to try to harm especially those of the "code users" who came into their bad books. They inform the administration, contrary to the prison regulations, about the behavior of "git people" and in this way bring down various repressions.

The "git people" act in the same way but more rarely. They try not to get in the way of the "fests" and especially of those who have unpaid jobs (trusties, recreation hall attendants). Some try to win a good reputation with the trusties or to cancel or recompensate the "crooked deeds." In order to achieve this goal, the "git people" can steal something whose disappearance would incriminate the trusty and then show him the place where the stolen object is hidden; by finding it, the trusty liquidates the threat hanging over him. He is grateful to his saviors and from that time on they will enjoy his support.

Neither the "fests" nor the "git people" "muck" a member of an antagonistic group directly. They are assisted by "victims" who sympathize with them and who, encouraged, "muck" the "fest" pointed out to them by the "git people" or the "git person" pointed out by the "fests."

Both groups have also eliminated the period of testing the newly arrived convicts ("America") which exists in other institutions. This period was used to see whether the novice was eligible for admittance to a given group. Now, the novices are immediately accepted by the group which they chose. The "fests" and the "git people" believe that the strength of a group depends, among other things, on the number of its members; hence, they compete for the novices. The rivalry starts after the arrival of new transports.

The novice is first registered by the administration. He is assigned to a cell and a cell block. After the initial formalities he is escorted to the building where he deposits his personal belongings and receives a prison outfit. In this building which is serviced by convicts—mainly the "fests"—the novice establishes his first contact with the inmates of the institution.

During their detention, the majority of the newcomers are informed about the divisions among the prisoners by experienced convicts, multiple offenders who have already served sentences. They find out about the "git people," "suckers" and "fags" but nothing, or almost nothing, about the "fests." The decisive majority of the convicts conveyed from detention to the penal institution are "code users." The rest are either unaffiliated or have been "suckered." In institution A it is established who is who. Those who have been "suckered" are included with the "victims." The "fests" try to draw the unaffiliated novices into their own group; if the newcomer refuses he could be "victimized." The "fests" also use various methods to force the "code users" to relinquish the "code" and to join the "fests" and threaten the novices with degradation. Such "victimization" by force is impossible if a guard[7] or a "git person" is nearby. Neither allows such a procedure although obviously for different reasons. In those situations the "fests" deal with the resistant newcomers by other methods, to which the guards or the "git people" do not react. In doing so, the "fests" reveal much ingenuity and cleverness. Let us imagine the novices standing in a row and reviewed by a functionary. A "fest" has approached the row from the back. He lightly taps one of the novices, whispers "hold it" into his ear and places on his outstretched hand a key which the novice drops in terror. But the others have already seen what occurred. "A person is not allowed to handle keys." In this way our newcomer has become a "victim." Another example: a key is thrown by a "fest" to a novice standing some distance away. The "fest" cries out: "Watch it." The novice catches the key by reflex. The others see the key in his hand, which turns him into a "victim."

Many of the novices manage to pass this stage without anyone attempting to force them to join the "fests." After their appearance in the cell, the novices who are still not affiliated are recruited by the "git people" and the "fests." In their capacity as "unvictimized," and after agreeing to belong to either the "fests" or the "git people," they instantly become members of the given group. Only a few are able to decide right away which group to choose. Both the "fests" and the "git people" try to convince the novices about the merits of belonging to their group and the losses connected with membership in the other groups. The novices avoid making a quick decision. They continue, however, to be subject to various forms of pressure and attempted enlistment.

An important element in these endeavors around the novice is the composition of the cell in which he has found himself. In cells dominated by the "git people" or the "fests," the novice as a rule becomes a member of the group which has more members. A "git person" who is placed in a cell outnumbered by "git people" retains his rank and finds support in his group. But a "git person" who finds himself in a cell of "fests" is forced by various methods to relinquish the "code" and to join the "fests." If he does not do so, then he is usually "degraded." The "fests" try by various means (persuasion, the threat of "mucking," beatings, cleaning up jobs) to force the "code user" to abandon the "code." Some, under this sort of pressure, cease to "use the code" and join the "fests."

Others, in order to "save face" often do not ask for admittance to the "fests." Consequently, they are "cursed" and become "victims." The refusal to join the "fests" in this situation can be brought about by fear of an eventual reprisal by the "git people." A lesser revenge hangs over the "victimized" person than over the few who relinquished the "code."

Some of the novices reject the proposals of both the "fests" and the "git people." They struggle to maintain their neutrality—"Switzerland." Sometimes the attainment of this position can be very difficult. A novice who lived in a cell with "code users" refused to become one of them and as a result was exploited and beaten. The "git people" also tried to force him to perform homosexual acts. At other times, by way of harassment, they threw him down on the floor and trampled on him. On still other occasions he was wrapped in a blanket and thrown up so high that he touched the ceiling ("push ups on the ceiling"). Of course, he was not allowed to sit at the table. Whenever he left the cell he was followed by one of the "git people" who checked whether he went in the direction he said he would. If he decided to go in a direction different than the one agreed upon, he was brought back to the cell and punished. The novice could not endure this state of permanent debasement and humiliation. One day, he used the opportunity of cleaning up an empty doctor's office and stole a large dose of medicine, which he swallowed. A moment later he lost consciousness. After undergoing medical treatment, he told the warden of institution A that he had had enough of living in the cell and requested to be moved to one with the "Swiss." Subsequently, he was transferred but here also found himself among "git people" and was treated as before. His reputation obviously followed him, passed on by the "people" from the first cell. After some time, the inmate once again decided to end his life. He brought a piece of window glass into the cell, and the next morning he did not go to work. Left all alone in the cell, he cut an artery of his neck and lay down on the bed, covered with a blanket. Some time passed before he was noticed by another convict who called for help. After returning from the hospital, the inmate notified the warden that he was ready to attempt suicide again, unless he was moved into a cell with the "Swiss." His request was granted, which gave him much satisfaction; henceforth, he described himself as a "Swiss" and claimed that he was "quite happy."

The "victims" maintain that they are better treated by the "fests" than by the "git people." In those cells where the latter constitute a majority, they often force the "victims" to clean up, they take the "victims' " food, steal their money and more valuable belongings, spit in their soup, and so forth. Neither do the "people" permit the "victim" to sit at the table. In workshops and schools the "people" force the "victims" to carry out all sorts of jobs, to work for them, and to meet the production quotas (the number of crates to be made during the workday by the convict). Sometimes, they extort finished products from the "victims" in order to reach the quota, or they exchange faulty products for good ones.

The "fests" treat the "victims" as inferior people and demonstrate their own superiority but exploit them much more rarely than do the "git people." Through all sorts of "deals" the "fests" arrange to get food, tea, and cigarettes and do not have to take them from the "victims." If they wish to compel the latter to do something they often pay them in cigarettes, or tea.

The "victims" can "muck" the "git people" who cause them suffering. The latter are afraid that a desperate "victim" could throw himself at them with a cloth dipped in the toilet bowl and "muck" them or do it in another fashion. Once a desperate "victim" defecated into a newspaper and entered a washroom full of "git people" upon whom he wished to revenge himself. He threw the newspaper and its contents in the direction of the "people" and, by splattering them, turned them into "victims," causing some to cry out and moan: "Jesus, I've stopped being git," while others slashed themselves.

A "victim" who is being harassed by certain "people" whose group he supports and whose leaders trust him can ask for intervention and protection from the members of that group. Szczepanek, a "victim," was well liked by the elite of the "people" from his ward and often kept their company. The "people" used his services but did so with sympathy and gentleness. In a sense he remained their good luck charm. At a certain stage two of the "people" of rather low standing among the "code users" began to annoy Szczepanek, who complained to the leaders. They, in turn, asked him to point out the guilty parties. Upon meeting them, they ordered them to stand still and urged Szczepanek to deliver blows. He then hit these live mannequins, spat on them and "cursed" them, thus turning them into "victims."

If the "victims" outnumber the "git people" in the cell, the former can harass the minority. They touch the dishes belonging to the "code users," making it impossible to use them since they become "unclean" and could be "harmful." A spoon or bowl handled by a "victim" cannot be used by a "git person." He is forced to throw them on the floor and smash them and is thus left with no utensils. If the "git people" ask the guards for new dishes, they can expect to be punished for destroying the old ones. The "victim" can also "break wind" during the meal, making it impossible for the "git people" to continue eating because the food has become "unclean."

The "Swiss" avoid all symptoms of strife between the groups and protect themselves against attempts at identifying them with the "victims."

The inmates exploit the "fags" for homosexual acts, usually bribing them with cigarettes or tea. The price depends on the act performed. The "fags" can masturbate the other inmates or they can sexually gratify them by means of oral or anal intercourse. Homosexual contact is sometimes initiated by the "fags" themselves. In return for cigarettes or tea they agree to be used as a source of sexual pleasure.

Relations within the group of the "git people"

At the beginning the "code users" do not treat the novice as a full fledged member of the group. The novice is provoked, threatened with assault and sometimes beaten—in other words, he is tested to see whether he will inform. It is permitted to appropriate his food and cigarettes, and he must never complain; otherwise he could fall into disgrace with the "people." If the newly arrived "git" convict manages to smuggle money into the cell after a visit, he is obliged to hand over a share to the "troublemaker" (the leader of the cell block). Otherwise, he might be assaulted and if he persists to refuse, the "git people" might "victimize" him.

Members who for a longer period of time do not adjust to the binding norms are rejected by the "git people" by being raped or forced to masturbate themselves or others. Sometimes the convicts are harassed to such an extent that they seek refuge in suicide or self-inflicted injuries. The "git people" settle the majority of accounts among themselves by a fist fight observed by the whole cell.

They also often violate their own rules. They do so in situations where the chances of being discovered are slight. For example, in solitary confinement cells they wash the toilet bowl with their hands. The "git people" are not allowed to eat after "police hour" (the announcement of a rest period) until the morning. Often, however, they break this rule. At night they steal the "victims'" food (although they are not allowed to handle things touched or used by the "victims" and "fags") and "grub it," of course in hiding. Those guilty of such misconduct do not admit to having performed it, fearing possible retaliation on the part of the leader of the cell block. Even if the leader finds out he usually issues an ultimatum: either the accused becomes a "victim" or he pays a fine out of the money received during the visiting period, before which he must write an illegal letter home requesting his family to provide the money. These letters are often dictated by the leader of the cell block. In them, the inmate implores his family, arguing that he is starving, has nothing to eat, drink or smoke. Sometimes the letters also contain blackmail. If the parents do not send the money, then the author of the letter will hang himself or, after release, will seek revenge. When the perpetrator hands over too little money, he becomes "victimized." Frequently, he has been "victimized" earlier and, upon delivery of the money, is "raised to the rank of a person" by the leader.

Another example illustrating conflicts within the group is provided by the following situation: a "git person" gave another "git person" 200 złoty for the purchase of six packages of tea. The second inmate, after buying the tea, gave it to another "git person" to pass it to the owner of the 200 złoty. The third convict did the same, and so on. Finally, the owner of the 200 złoty received only three "drawers" of tea (a "drawer" = a matchbox), in other words, two-thirds of a single package. The original purchaser explained that each of the intermediaries had to receive his "share" for taking the risk. The owner of the 200 złoty was helpless, and if he insisted on complaining, he could "fall down" (be degraded or raped).

The "git person" who has disgraced himself and is either very strong or "knows too much" usually avoids "falling down." A borrows money from B (both "git people") and if A does not return the money in time, he is usually victimized. But if A "knows too much" then no action is taken since he could revenge himself by relaying to the administration information detrimental to the more important members of the group. He could also be "protected" by his friends.

"Git people" help their friends when they find themselves in a difficult situation; for instance, they pass cigarettes or food to inmates in solitary confinement, or they organize riots, or begin hunger strikes, if their friend is being harmed.

Frequently "git people" denounce other members of their own group to the administration. They bully younger and weaker members by taking their food and "cursing" them, while the victims must annul the "curses" by using special plays on words. The "git people" even permit one of their own to clean the shoes of another. They cruelly joke among themselves: by throwing a jar of vaseline under the feet of a person entering the cell in such a way that he does not notice it and walks over the jar, they turn him to a "victim," since he should have kicked it aside.

Relations within the group of the "Swiss," "victims," and "fags"

None of these groups is as integrated as the "fests" or the "git people." The "Swiss" take care not to be accidentally included among the "victims," the "victims" take care not to become "fags." Within these categories of prisoners there are also several score of "waffleshops."

The "Swiss" believe that everyone may do as he likes and are concerned only with their own welfare. They have no obligations toward members of their own group and if one of them antagonizes the "git people" or the "fests," they begin treating him as a "victim." All three groups exploit each other; the strongest or cleverest one wins. As a rule, each of the "Swiss," "victims," or "fags" sympathizes with the "fests" or the "git people."

Sometimes new spontaneous and short-lived groups appear among the "victims," with members called for example "bangladesh," "je t'aime," or "teges." They involve a small percentage of the "victims" and constitute groups of friends which, in periods of greater cohesion, take on names ("bangladesh" and "je t'aime" from songs fashionable at one time and "teges" because its members added the meaningless word "teges" to each sentence).

Relations within the "fest" group

The novices in the groups of trusties go through a trial period. During this time they are supposed to learn the principles of conduct and speech. The "fests" attach greater importance to linguistic training than do the "git people." If, for example, a convict says "move yourself" instead of "shift yourself" he will be slapped on the head. Those who pass the trial period successfully are initiated and become full-fledged members of the group. They cease being exploited and feel much safer in their group than their counterparts in the "git people."

Expulsions from the group occur when a certain "fest" gets involved in affairs which, in the eyes of the other "fests," should not interest him.

This includes "settling" tea, cigarettes, and food. Self-interest is very important for the "fests." It must be respected and guarded lest some unentitled person penetrate it; if others know too much, the situation becomes dangerous. The group condemns theft among its own members and immediately casts the offender from its ranks.

The "fests" win the trust of the administration and in this way are assigned to profitable assignments: trusties, recreation hall attendants, good work in the production enterprise, and the like. These job assignments create favorable conditions for "deals" concerning various articles. Members of the group who hold these profitable posts are as a rule leaders of the group. They share consumer goods with their helpers and with sympathizing members from their own group, as well as with those "victims" with whom they have joint interests.

The important "fests" observe the principles of conduct and consistently call for their observance by other members. Their approach in this issue is, however, deprived of the emotional involvement typical for other groups. They treat all "fests" favorably with the exception of those who are going through the trial period.

In settling accounts the "fests" use undercover methods: they inform the administration about their enemies, usually offering false and harmful information. As a group they also do not help members who are penalized for refusing to work and fulfilling duties. In other cases, the "fests" assist each other, unless help calls for an excessive risk.

Sources of illegal profit

1. The prisoners produce many articles illegally. The variety and quality of those products depends on the raw material and tools available in the penal institutions and on the skills of the inmates themselves. One can distinguish three types of articles, from the point of view of their functions or purpose:

a. personal use: knives, cigarette lighters, matchboxes, cigarette cases, wallets, decorated picture frames for family photographs, ornaments (chains, crosses, etc.),

b. products of their own creative expression: poems, songs, stories, drawings, patterns for tattoos,

c. articles intended for trade: wooden boxes lined with straw, candlesticks, flower pot stands, masks made from synthetic material and paper, pictures from colored magazines glued onto pieces of wood, flat pieces of wood decorated with various burned out (carved) patterns.

This type of production, however, is not very considerable because of a limited access to raw materials and tools, and often because of the prisoners' lack of skill.

The articles are purchased by prison employees or the "free" workers (those not employed in the prison administration—teachers or workers in the prison). In turn, the inmates receive money, tea, food, or, more rarely, vodka. The production of the above mentioned articles calls for raw material and uncomplicated tools, which can be obtained only by a suitable position at work or doing some sort of an unpaid job. The majority of these profitable posts are held by the "fests." They also have better contact with the administration (whose trust they enjoy) and are scrutinized to a much lesser degree.

2. During the visiting period, their families sometimes give them money, which they swallow in such a way as not to be seen by the guards; after being searched and upon their return to the cells they vomit the money out.

3. The inmates send letters home via some of the workers, mainly the "free" ones, asking their families to reply to the address of these employees. The latter deliver the money or purchased articles (tea, cigarettes) to the convicts and usually take part of the sum as gratuity. The condition necessary for making such transactions is a close rapport between the inmates and the employees, which is the type of contact established mainly by the "fests."

4. Prisoners who have a given profession (there are but a few in institution A) and can, for example, repair household appliances, are employed by the administration (unofficially) to perform various services (e.g., the repair of a vacuum cleaner); in return, they receive privileges or material gratuities such as money, tea, and cigarettes.

I have indicated sources of the illegal income of the workers outside the prison community, which I will call external. Now, I will discuss the *internal* sources, i.e., various ways of obtaining goods by the prisoners from other inmates. Generally these internal sources can be divided into two varieties:

1. The first are those resulting from the existence of groups ("git people" and "fests"), the protection of their interests, the normative system obligatory for their members, laws, customs, etc.

• New members of a group must buy their way in, offer money or food to the important members of the group; they must also share money obtained illegally (for example, during visits) with other members of the group. This custom is observed mainly among the "people."

• The "victims" who wish to be accepted by the "people" must pay the leaders of the group a certain sum of money.

• "People" who have broken the rules of the group (a fact of which other "people" are aware) and who do not want to be expelled may be obliged by the leaders to pay money or hand over, for example, a certain amount of tea (these cases are rare among the "fests").

• The violation of norms by a member of the group may become the reason for blackmailing that member by another one who has witnessed the misconduct.

• Stealing or extortion from the "victims" food (tea) and cigarettes by the "people" is almost universal.

• The group allows the exploitation of other prisoners (from outside the group) and often supports this type of act by those members who share their spoils.

• Bribery: "fests," who, for example, wish to bring about the expulsion of an inmate from the "git people," pay a "victim" to "muck" him.

• Prisoners who belong to a concrete social category determine what sort of services are to be performed by whom and for whom. Basically, both the "fests" and the "people" force the "victims" to carry out diverse services and they profit from the work performed by the "victim." The "fests," however, use fewer threats. As a rule, they pay with tea or cigarettes (they can afford to do so since they are wealthier than the "people"). Nor do they profit as much from the services performed for them by the "victims." These services include laundering underwear; cleaning cells (including toilet bowls); sewing and darning; concessions to the "people" in all circumstances (for example, exchanging better beds for worse ones); meeting the work norms in place of the "people"; and accepting penalties for the violation of the prison rules by the "people."

2. Other sources of obtaining goods internally are not directly linked with the existence of the division into groups: theft; reselling of various goods; sharing goods with one's colleagues (so-called waffles); profits from performing services (for example, school assignments, tattooing, writing official pleas, cutting hair); and loans.

Illegal Production and Trade: "Hidden Life" *without an Unwritten Code*

Already during their first stay in prison the recidivists incarcerated in institution B came into contact with "hidden life." It was also then that the prisoners' community ascribed them to a certain social category, and they were or would become members of that same category in successive institutions. "Hidden life" seems to be introduced into institution B and reactivated by the multiple offenders. Therefore, one cannot speak about the emergence of an informal structure of the prisoners' community but rather about its transformations.

I had considerable difficulties trying to identify the divisions among the prisoners in institution B and to describe the code that regulates their conduct. In the first place, although the inmates were familiar with the terms "fag," "sucker," "person," and "fest," the community did not demonstrate a greater interest in determining who was who. I encountered inmates who said that they themselves were "people," and that there were other "people," but they were unable to point them out. Similarly, while not able to point out "suckers," they were unable to unambiguously describe either "suckers" or "people." In other words, I did not observe a strong tendency toward stratification or polarization.

Secondly, those who described themselves as "people" claimed that they were not particularly concerned with what others thought of them and who they were. They were "people" "for themselves," and kept the company of those whom they regarded as "people." Let me add that not everyone who claimed to be a "person" was a member of the "people" for the others. The "people" "kept together" in small groups of friends.

Thirdly, there was no one in this community who could be viewed as the head of the "people." In the past, certain inmates were regarded as leaders and even exercised power over the "people." But later on, according to the prisoners, the administration "destroyed" or transferred them to another prison. Some leaders were "mucked" by the "people" when it became apparent that they had cooperated with the administration.

Fourthly, there supposedly exists an unwritten code of conduct for the "people" which in reality they often broke with no subsequent consequences.

Fifthly, some of the inmates knew that other inmates spoke of them as "suckers" but "refused to do anything about this." They were not particularly afraid of the "people" and maintained that actually there is no "code" at all "nor the divisions which exist among the juveniles." "We had a case here when some so-called sucker was serving dinner and poured soup into the bowls; one of the 'code users' did not want to hand him his bowl because he does not take anything from a 'sucker.' Then this 'sucker' slugged him so forcefully with a large serving spoon that the other one fell back into the cell. From then on he took his meals from 'suckers.' The guard who was there at the time just laughed.''

What is relevant in presenting the structure of the prisoners' community in institution B is to demonstrate its difference from those already familiar to us—and based on an unwritten code which regulates the behavior of the inmates. More so in order to meet the requirements of formalities than to express the essence of that which is the heart of the matter with regard to the prisoners' community in institution B, we will begin with remnants of the classical form of "hidden life" which to a rather small degree rules the conduct of the inmates.

Residues of the classical form of "hidden life"

The main norms binding for the "people" are:
1. It is forbidden to take the passive role in homosexual acts.
2. It is forbidden to inform.
3. It is forbidden to exploit another "person."
4. A "person" is expelled from the group for breaking norms.
Other norms proclaim that:
1. It is forbidden to deal with "suckers."
2. A "person" does not have to fight with a "sucker" even if the latter provokes him, but he must fight if he is provoked by another "person."
3. It is forbidden to kick during a fight.
4. It is forbidden to accept a cigarette held by a "fag" but it is permitted to take one from a pack.
5. It is forbidden to shake hands with a "sucker," a "fag" or a "screw."
6. Close rapport with a "fag" is suspicious and can harm a "person."

The "people" can "set a 'sucker' straight" and admit him into their group. In return he pays a certain sum of money or offers tea or vodka. The size of the sum demanded by the "people" depends on the situation of the "sucker" and varies from one to 2,000 złoty; "if you have money, then you are a 'git person.' " The "people" do not constitute an integrated group—there is no leader or structure of power. They function in smaller or larger groups, do "deals" together, and offer mutual support.

The "people" maintain that the "suckers" are impractical and not very clever. In their opinion a "sucker" is predestined for financial and material exploitation. A "sucker" is a person who: is "cursed" by the "people''; informs or is suspected of doing so; was exploited financially or materially ("is turned over'').

"Fags'' are those inmates who were raped by their fellow prisoners. Nonetheless, in order to become a "fag'' it is sometimes sufficient to "be paid out'' or "pissed on.'' One can distinguish four categories:

1. Those who "sell'' themselves to everyone in return for such gratuities as tea, cigarettes, or money (homosexual prostitution).

2. Those who "surrender'' themselves only to one prisoner (and remain faithful).

3. Those who were raped but are not homosexuals.

4. Those who were "paid out'' or "pissed on.''

In institution B all the "fags'' are treated identically; they are not allowed to share a table nor are there any social contacts. A "fag'' always remains a "fag'' and neither he nor anyone else is capable of changing this state of affairs.

One of the "fags'' was a tall and well-built man who in the opinion of the inmates was one of the strongest men in the institution. He never engaged in homosexual acts, which probably repelled him, but had become a "fag'' as a young boy in a reformatory. Despite his prowess and avoidance of homosexual intercourse (even as the active party), he could not change his status. One day, he beat up and chased away some "git people'' who had bullied him. They began looking for help among other "people'' but no one came to their assistance since no one wanted to deal with this immensely strong man. Nonetheless, despite his physical advantage, he remained a "fag'' and was treated as one as long as it was possible.

Inmates whose social category is unknown are described here as "unidentified.'' It should be understood that many prisoners do not show any initiative to identify themselves with a given social category. Neither do the remaining inmates care to establish "who they are'' nor ascribe themselves to any specific social category.

Indices of the transformation of structures in the prisoners' community

"HIDDEN LIFE'' IN THE ESTIMATION OF THE PRISONERS

"This is a jungle.'' "There is no solidarity.'' "Money is regarded higher than strength.'' "Honor, ambition . . . both remain at the very bottom of the hierarchy of values." "If you have the money then you're a 'git person' and when you no longer have any, you will once again become a 'sucker.' " "Every one worries about himself and no one cares who is who (a 'person' or a 'sucker')." "I committed this crime by myself, I sit here by myself, and will leave by myself." "Here the person who stands well (financially) and who has strong fists is important."

Some of the prisoners view others as "people," but the latter do not consider themselves as such and say that they "are above and beyond all that." In turn, a number of inmates consider themselves to be "people" but the "people" do not accept them. "I belonged to the 'people,' but they do not acknowledge that here. They cheat each other. There are groups, each of several persons, who keep together. Apart from them no one is considered important." "I don't want to use their language. I have my own opinions." "I used the code some time ago . . . and it just stayed that way." "I stopped using the code and . . . no longer do it." "I belong to the 'code users' . . . but nowadays it is not the same, the norms are no longer rigidly observed. I have my honor and ambition. None of the guards want to do deals with the 'people,' no one wants to talk to them." "The code used to exist in the past, now it is gone. It no longer pays. It has become accepted not to squeal. The 'people' don't have leaders, everyone governs himself." Many of the "people" who maintain contacts with the "suckers," as long as they are profitable, are described as those who "carry."

"AFFAIRS"

A "person" who for some reason has a grudge against another "person" tries to involve him in an "affair." The "involvement in affairs" is composed of two states:

1. A "person" spreads a rumor, for example, that another "person" is a concealed "fag" or informer and does so in such a way as to make it difficult to determine the source of the rumor.

2. The reputation of the "person" who is being "involved in an affair" is already suitably prepared among the "people." None of them wish to have anything to do with the suspect. The latter notices this change of attitude, alters his own conduct, and becomes wary and sensitive. Such behavior confirms the suspicions of the others which, simultaneously, turns into a conviction about their correctness. The victim is then expelled from the group and labeled as a "sucker."

"DEGRADATION INTO A 'FAG' "

The "people" are bound by a norm which says that they may not exploit another "person." A "person" who borrows money is obliged to return it after a given period of time. He can spend the money on tea or vodka or lose it in a card game, etc. If there is no possibility of winning it back and returning it, then the borrower is faced with the possibility that the lender will inform his friends and together they will beat him up. The only solution is to turn the creditor into a "sucker" who has no right to demand the return of the money. The way to do this is to insult him in such a way as to degrade him. This inability to return a debt is often the reason for "involvement in an affair," and if the "affair" is arranged suitably, there is no need to use any other methods.

A "person" who borrows money and has no opportunity to get it back or to punish the debtor becomes a "sucker" and an object of jokes, since "he who allows himself to be cheated is a 'sucker.' "

"EMBASSY"

Both the "people and the "suckers" frequently apply for unpaid jobs in the prison. They accept such jobs as cooks, barbers, school janitors, librarians, orderlies, or editors in the prison radio network. The number of these posts is limited, and the opportunity for obtaining them is enjoyed only by those inmates who are trusted and known for their good conduct (in the eyes of the administration). These jobs create for the select few a chance for closer contact with the workers and for bartering for tea and cigarettes in return for money, products, or services. The inmates who hold the unpaid jobs are called "ambassadors" by the other prisoners. After the morning roll call, the "ambassadors" go to their jobs; they are free from the prison regime and surveillance which affect the remaining inmates. They can also move freely in their workplaces and are rarely controlled. They do not have to sit in the cell after working hours, and their cells are rarely searched. The "ambassadors" also receive rewards more often and their appeals for conditional discharge are supported. The administration treats them more leniently, and they are rarely victims of verbal or physical aggression.

When a year ago S arrived in institution B, he made it known that he was a "git person." He was also of the opinion that institution B should be governed by the "people" who must make "order." But when less than a year later he became an "ambassador" and was asked whether he had also ceased to "use the code," he answered that he "uses it for himself" and not for the "others." His own convictions which he regarded as the "code" did not interfere in being part of the "embassy." Immediately after discharge from the penal institution of one of the "corridor men" (responsible for order in the corridor), S bribed the other "corridor men" so that they would propose his candidacy for this post to the guards. Having received the job, he also paid a certain sum to one of the guards.

"TEA DRINKERS"

A "tea drinker" is a colleague from the cell with whom an inmate drinks tea. The tea made here, similar to the one in institution A, is a strong extract. Joint tea drinking denotes the existence of friendship. The "tea drinkers" share property and help each other. "Tea drinking" can involve more than two persons—sometimes three or even four. Joint consumption constitutes a basis for distinguishing this particular group since tea is never taken with others.

"COUNTRYMEN"

The foundation of closer ties between the convicts is their origin from the same part of the country, the same town, district, or village. The "countrymen" keep together, assist each other, defend their own in case of attacks by other inmates, together obtain various articles, trade, etc. If two or more "countrymen" stay in one cell they can become "tea drinkers." In institution B the "tea drinkers" could include a "person" and a "sucker" (especially when the "sucker" possesses money or various commodities) and this type of division ceases to be important. On the basis of the links between "countrymen," cooperation between "suckers" and "people" was also possible in order to gain goods or to offer help.

In the past the "countrymen" links in institution B provided the underlying foundation for the emergence of groups of prisoners who "had the most to say" and "ruled the prison." "Sometimes power was held by the wise guys (from Warsaw) but later they were replaced by the kangaroos (from Szezecin)," groups which monopolized illegal production and trade.

THE PROTECTION OF TRADE

Illicit production and trade are the objects of surveillance by the authorities in the institution. But the prisoners are concerned with the protection of production and commodities ("faience"). This protection involves contacts with "screws" and free employees with whom the inmates barter. Each "bad break" is analyzed and categorized as either a case of informing or as an accident. If the first possibility was the cause, then the prisoners attempt to discover the "squealer." The suspect is then "tested." In one example, four of the "people" met without the person suspected of "selling" the fifth member of the group. They established that in his presence one of them would inform the whole group, which usually did "deals" together, that guard X would supply half a liter of spirits on the following day. They also decided that from that moment, in order to exclude the possibility of suspecting someone else from the group, all four would stay together until the end of the next day and never lose sight of each other. If it turned out that the guard was under surveillance, then the suspect, uncontrolled by his peers and unaware of the trap, would in fact inform.

On the following day the inmates found out that "screw" X was searched upon entering the institution. Since nothing was found, the guards who performed the search apologized, referring to "false information" they had received about alcohol that was to be smuggled in. The four "people" took under consideration the possibility that this incident was an accident. In order to check further, they applied, to use their own words, a "test of reaction to an accusation": when all five were alone in their cell, one of the above mentioned four turned to the suspect and said "You cock"; the others observed his reaction. In such a situation a real "person would begin a fight with the one who 'cursed' him. But if he is guilty and has something on his conscience, then he will break down." The suspected inmate actually did break down and "sobbed and begged" not to be beaten. His reaction "spoke for itself," and he admitted to the charges.

Since the administration condemned homosexual rape, the inmates forwent this form of degradation and substituted a "pay out." In this case they struck the informer's forehead and neck with their penises. The news of the degradation spread rapidly. Within twenty-four hours, the administration transferred the victim to another prison "at the other end of

Poland," expecting that it would take longer for information about him to reach the new institution. Despite the fact that everyone including the administration knew that the penalized convict was "degraded to a fag" and knew who had performed the degradation, the victim never informed the administration officially, and therefore it was impossible to take sanctions against the perpetrators.

The most sought after articles are tea, cigarettes, vodka, and food. Of course, the possession and drinking of tea or vodka are strictly forbidden—tea can be drunk only when it is served with meals. One can speak about an addiction to tea and tobacco among almost all the inmates; tea and cigarettes stifle hunger and nervousness ("if one is hungry then it's good to light up or take some tea [they use the Russian word] and calm the nerves"). The prisoners try to obtain and store as much tea and cigarettes as possible. Apart from consumption, these articles also serve as a medium of exchange in paying for the services of other inmates: passing messages outside the prison, purchasing lighters, etc. The inmates try to have good relations with those among them who own these goods, or at least they pretend that these relations are good. One can always borrow or purchase articles or obtain them for performing a service. Often, one can simply get them for nothing, since the owners support the other inmates. But most often they demand obedience or support in return. Those inmates who receive cigarettes and tea at their own request, or are offered them "out of pity," are said to "to start on a crooked snout" or "sit on a trailer."

Prisoner R was regarded by some as a "sucker." He was a "peddler," and in return for tea, cigarettes, money, etc., he sold articles produced illegally by the prisoners to the administration. He owned so much that he was able to buy up the "faience" from the prisoners without worrying about the actual buyer. Prisoner J, with whom R shared a cell, is a "sucker"; he used to be a "fest" in institution A and now he is described as a "fest after a cock," in other words, he has been "cursed." Some time ago R and J were tea drinkers, but now their relations have deteriorated and R denies J the use of the table and accuses him of being a "crooked snout." "Let him make deals himself since he is so sure of himself."

Sometimes "crooked snouts" include inmates who describe themselves as "people," while among the owners of goods are prisoners who are called "suckers."

In order to obtain the desirable goods, a prisoner must sometimes enter into trade relations with another inmate or a whole group of prisoners who are treated in a hostile way by his own group. Therefore, he must remain very careful and conceal his close relations with his profitable trading partners: prisoner K, maintains R, pretends to be a "git person" in his place of work and keeps the company of the "people." This is ridiculous, adds R, since K delivers to him the "faience" he produces and is very satisfied with the payments—good relations with R matter to him very much. K plays the role of R's great friend, fulfills his orders, and curries favor. R says that K is "carried" and wants to "have it good here and there."

"THE DEPARTMENT FOR LOAFERS"

In institution B one of the cell blocks is intended for the non-working inmates who for various reasons are unable to work in the prison enterprise. Presence in this cell block, of course, means a total loss of opportunities to earn money. The reasons for placing prisoners here include:

1. poor health
2. tendencies toward heading an informal organization of prisoners and the organization and development of "hidden life"
3. insufficient places of work or the lack of skills or qualifications on the part of the prisoner
4. improper behavior at work (so-called bad attitude toward work) or neglect of duties.

Prisoners housed in the cell block for "loafers" are isolated and spend their whole time within the bounds of the institution. They carry out various unpaid work for the administration, and the chances for illegal production or barter are almost nonexistent. "Here they live off what is passed to them." They are hungry and are sent no tea or cigarettes by colleagues from those cell blocks where the opportunity to "arrange" these commodities is much greater. External sources of illicit income are extremely limited, and the dominating internal ways resemble those in institution A.

In this particular cell block, a distinctly outlined division into "people," "fags," and "suckers" exists, which is consistently observed. The "hidden life" here brings to mind the classical descriptions of that phenomenon.

Reasons for changes in the structure
of the prisoners' community

The primary illegal source of the prisoners' income is the production of articles for everyday use. By making use of the tools and raw materials available in the prison enterprises, the inmates make: notebooks, candlesticks, rings, necklaces, folding television tables, wall lamps, albums, cigarette cases, switchblade knives, pictures (canvas and straw in a frame), hunting knives, axes, cleavers, table ware, and stiletto knives. These articles are bought by the "screws" who, once their own personal needs are satisfied, distribute them in the nearby town. The variety of objects produced changes according to the demand of the local market.

The prison enterprise workshop has many machines and tools: lathes, milling and grinding machines, metal saws, tubs for nickeling and chrome coating, each of which is manned by the inmates. Here an inmate who plans to illegally produce and later sell some article must cooperate with other prisoners working at their machines. For example, the production of a switchblade knife means not only obtaining suitable material but also access to various machines and the ability to work them. It is therefore necessary to communicate with colleagues and to ask them to produce some element or to tool it in a given way. In return, they share the profit from the sale; the prisoner can also undertake to make an element needed by his colleagues who are unable to produce a certain article all by themselves. Such production is feasible only with the use of many machines and tools.

Illegal production would be impossible if the prisoners' community consistently observed the divisions into "people" and "suckers" as well as the norms and principles inducing the "people" to reject cooperation with the "suckers" and permitting them to beat, exploit, and suppress them. The "suckers" could refuse to cooperate, block access to their machines, and refuse to tool the products. The "people" thus must forget about divisions and principles; they are concerned with profits from illegal production, just as they must share profits with "suckers" participating in the production of the sold articles. Such cooperation becomes for quite a few "people" more valuable than an unprofitable contact with another "person."

Not only production bonds but also those which are generated by the process of trafficking in illicitly produced articles contribute to the disappearance of the social structure based on the division between "people" and "suckers." If a prisoner wishes to sell a switchblade knife to a "screw" who works in the prison pavilion, he must first deliver the item. Upon entering the pavilion he is searched. The inmates claim that about 50 percent of the illegally produced articles are lost at this stage. The "screws" rarely report illegal production and smuggling of articles. Usually they pass in silence over such incidents and appropriate goods. Some, however, prepare reports, adding as evidence the item discovered during the search. Others confiscate the article, and when questioned by their superior, answer that it was lost or thrown out. In order to avoid such losses, the inmates could try to come to a tacit understanding with the "screws" who conduct the search, but this is a risky undertaking. Even if the "screw" agrees to such cooperation, he may actually carry out the search anyway. Moreover, a prisoner who makes such a proposal could "become marked" and in the future be subjected to constant searches. This is why only some of the inmates decide to take this step. Others take the risk by counting on not being searched or not thoroughly enough, or they rely on the tolerance of the functionaries. The safest way, however, is to hand over products to those inmates who for various reasons are not searched by the "screws" (those who inform, bribe the guards, etc.). Of course, this procedure is accompanied by an additional division of the profits.

In the prison itself the producer regains the "faience"[8] and can sell it to one of the employees. There is not always, however, a buyer waiting; one must be found. Once again an intermediary is needed, who as a rule is one of the prisoners working as "ambassadors" (the group that enjoys best contacts with the "screws" and has opportunities for safely storing the "faience" in the library, school, or recreation hall where they work). Certain functions allow the ambassadors to move around the prison. The inmate who delivers newspapers to all the pavilions can distribute "faience," money, or tea and reach the prisoners or the administration workers; the school janitor can receive the "faience" and, after selling it, pass the tea to the owner. Of course, the entire process of production and trade contains the risk of a "bad break" which, however, is diminished by the following factors:

1. The "screw" can confiscate the "faience" for himself, in which case he is unlikely to report the incident;

2. The "screw" knows that the "faience" will be sold to one of the workers, who could be his own colleague or superior; therefore, he will not confiscate the commodity but will take the risk that someone else will

search the prison, in which case he will be held responsible only for neglecting his duties;

3. The "screws" simply do not feel like searching all the prisoners,
since this takes too much time;

4. The "screws" do not want to antagonize the inmates by their over-
eagerness, since they too, after all, may "make life difficult" or, for instance, refuse to produce "faience."

A network of producers and peddlers develops. The inmate produces,
the mediator passes, and the trader buys and sells the "faience." Sometimes all these functions or most of them are performed by the same person, in this manner increasing the profits. Of course, in order for
production and trade to be at all feasible, no importance can be attached
to the social division of the community into "people" and "suckers,"
which would make impossible or at least hinder both production and barter, and thus the earnings.

Illegal production and trade based on it is not the only opportunity for
additional income. Other sources assist the process of transforming the
structure of the inmates' community and molding relations on the basis of
an illicit market.

• Many of the prisoners have a profession which they learned previously. Sometimes their skills are utilized by the administration. They perform certain jobs for the prison itself (maintenance, repairs) and for the
workers of the administration. These professions include tinsmiths (auto
body repair), painters, carpenters, electricians (repair of installations, vacuum cleaners, etc.), radio-television technicians. In return the administrative workers offer money, articles much sought by the inmates (tea,
cigarettes, sometimes vodka), rewards (e.g., an additional ration card for
food in the prison canteen), promises of conditional release.

• Some of the inmates show considerable manual skill. They produce
various bric-a-brac (miniature pianos, compacts, boxes) out of raw material available in the prison or supplied by the administration. These articles then become objects of an exchange between their producers and the
"screws."

• Prisoners who enjoy closer contact with some of the functionaries of
the prison staff or "free" workers (teachers, employees in the production
enterprises) are able to send letters to their families or acquaintances with
requests for money to be forwarded to the home addresses of the penitentiary staff member. After receiving the money, the functionary puts some
aside for himself (for "the risk taken," or for the "effort," usually 50 per-

cent of the sum) and delivers the rest to the inmate. Instead of money he may bring food, if such an agreement was made earlier. Of course, this cooperation is illegal and kept undercover by the inmates and personnel participating in it. On one occasion the "people" collected the addresses of other convicts and in their names forwarded requests for money, for example claiming that the convict himself was unable to write because he was in solitary confinement and that in order to get out he must bribe the "screw." These letters were then sent by the administrative workers who took their share of the money and gave the rest to the inmate, who, in turn, divided it among all those who aided him in collecting the addresses.

• During family visits, the prisoners swallow bank notes which, after being searched and returning to their cells, they vomit and thus regain.

• Some of the inmates employed in the prison enterprises steal work clothes, tools, raw materials, etc. (e.g., hide) and sell them to the workers of the administration who, because of their functions and places of work, do not have such opportunities.

• Certain material gratuities are given by the administration to those inmates who inform.

In addition to these *external* (outside the boundaries of the prison community) sources for obtaining money and consumer goods, there are *internal* sources based on the general monetary and commodity wealth owned by the inmates: cards, dominoes, etc., for money or tea; interest from loans (money, tea, etc.); "smuggling" (described previously); theft; sharing food with a "tea drinker" or "countryman"; soccer pools.

In the last case four prisoners (who are regarded as honest and efficient) are chosen to be the bankers (they often offer their services themselves, but they must be accepted by the others). The inmates present to the banker the scores of the results of a forthcoming soccer match together with an appropriate amount of tea. The banker makes a suitable chart of the results and the rates (tea or money) and takes 10 percent of the general deposit. A player has the right to demand that the banker make a copy of the expected results and paid rates—at a price of 10 packages of tea. The winner usually allots one quarter of his winnings for the next game. If the winnings are considerable, he may sell a large part of the tea or give it to his friends.

• The "fags" (homosexual prostitutes) accept payment (tea, cigarettes) for intercourse or masturbating the client. A homosexual faithful to one prisoner becomes his kept lover. Sometimes a "fag" blackmails inmates—for example, he demands cigarettes and when refused warns that he will begin to shout that he is being raped. If still refused, he starts to tear his own clothes and scream. The "screw," hearing the false accusations, might punish the inmates accused of rape, unless he sees through the fictional situation. If, however, the "screw" dislikes the suspect, he eagerly uses the situation for further harassment, even if he guesses the truth.

• Instances of buying "the rank of a person" by "suckers."

• Those prisoners who give part of their food to their colleagues (as a rule to those who have no opportunities of obtaining the goods) request in return support and aid, especially in a conflict with other inmates.

Yet Another "Hidden Life"

The institution houses inmates who have at most three to five years left of their terms and thus have served time in closed penal institutions where they were assigned by the prison community to a certain social category. Thus the structure of the "hidden life" is introduced into institution C by the inmates themselves. Just as in the case of institution B, we cannot speak about the emergence of an informal social structure of prisoners, but rather about its transformations:

• code users (people)
• non-code users
• fags

"People" and the main binding norms

A "person" cannot exploit another "person"; the "people" are not allowed to inform; a "person" cannot play a passive role in homosexual intercourse; the "people" are not allowed to cooperate with the administration (to fulfill unpaid functions).

In each cell block the "people" have their leader who, together with his assistants, decides who is to be expelled from the group and what attitude is to be taken toward the various decisions of the administration or the events within the inmates' community (for example, the departure from the "people" of one of their members). The "people" do not eat at the same time with other convicts ("non-people") but accept meals served by the "non-people" with the exception of the "fags."

The "non-code users"

Those convicts who do not belong to the "people" are called "non-code users"; they remain indifferent to the principles observed by the "code users," claiming that the two groups are identical, "only the code users isolate themselves from us." The "non-code users" have no principles of their own, although they stress that informing is forbidden. They also do not establish partner-like contacts with the "fags."

The "code users" and the "non-code users" maintain mutual contacts (although sometimes secret). They talk with each other and hold positive opinions about each other. "The 'non-code users' do not disturb me as long as they don't denounce. I have friends among them."

The "code users" are hostile toward the "non-code users" who work for the administration (this concerns the unpaid work of the inmates) and believe that they inform. They also have no contacts with the "fags" and even "eradicate them." In institution C the number of "fags" is small, and there are none at all in certain cell blocks; hence, the problem is almost nonexistent.

There is also no exploitation of the "non-code users" by the "code users." Consumer goods are obtained via trade transactions. Exploitation does take place sometimes among the "people" themselves: the "head" of the "people," for example, can take the tea of another "person." Individual members have been known to leave the group.

A "code user" who abandons the group is usually assaulted by the "people." He rationalizes his step by the lack of profits from belonging to the group, a desire to make his own decisions, and a greater opportunity for obtaining conditional release (the administration is unwilling to support motions for the conditional discharge of inmates belonging to the "people").

Sources of illegal income

For eight to ten hours a day the prisoners stay outside the limits of the institution (with the exception of Sundays). They work in different enterprises in the nearby region, where their superiors are the local workers. The jobs performed by the inmates are also monitored by the prison staff whose duty is to control periodically (the patrol system). Nonetheless, control over the inmates in the place of work is much less than in the penal institution. This creates opportunities for winning sought-after goods in various ways.

1. The inmates willingly undertake additional production tasks (apart from those which they are obliged to execute), intended for the civil workers, in return for money, tea, vodka, and other goods.

2. The inmates illicitly sell raw materials, tools, or finished products to chance acquaintances (and to the "screws"); for example, in the sawmill they sell timber, in the cement works they sell cement, and those building roads traffick in picks, spades.

3. The presence of inmates outside the institution and the absence of scrutiny make it possible for the civilian employees of the prison enterprises and for the prison staff to hire the prisoners for their own private purposes (for example, to build a trailer or a house) for which the inmates receive payment.

4. Often, the prisoners are offered various articles (cigarettes, tea, food, vodka) from the civilian employees as a treat or gift intended for people living in dire conditions.

5. The prisoners send letters requesting money, to their families via the workers who then pass on the money forwarded to their addresses (sometimes profiting from this procedure).

6. Such correspondence also makes it possible to arrange a meeting with the family (often with the help of the civilian workers) and then to obtain the desired goods directly.

Contact with ordinary workers of various enterprises also creates an opportunity for meeting women. It is difficult to estimate how widespread are the sexual relations between prisoners and the workers of a given enterprise (or chance acquaintances), but they certainly take place.

The goods obtained are usually consumed in the workplace—transportation to the penal institution is much too hazardous. Access to the goods, via the employees of the enterprise, is universal. It depends on the cunning and talent for striking up acquaintances. The inmates no longer depend on themselves. They help each other (for example, by quickly loading timber onto the wagon of a "shady" client) and divide the profit. People with freedom do not understand the division of the inmates into "code users" and "non-code users" and treat all the prisoners the same. For instance, they offer vodka and do not take into consideration that the inmates are members of different social categories, compelling them to drink together.

Keeping to the traditional rules and customs of the penal institution would make the consumption of the goods impossible.

In contrast to prisoners from institution B, those from institution C do not acquire illegal articles through a large number of intermediaries. The whole procedure is usually performed directly by the inmate and the person from outside.

The Meaning of Access to Goods and the Way of Gaining Them for the Structure of the Prisoners' Community

The "deprivation" model versus the "importation" model of the origin of "hidden life"

The debate about whether "hidden life" emerges in prison or is brought in by the felons has been present in pertinent literature almost from the appearance of works on the topic. According to some scholars, "hidden life" is a consequence of the pain generated by prison confinement, a form of social reaction to the deprivation of needs resulting from incarceration.[9] Others, while more or less accepting this position, maintain that "hidden life" is imported from the outside into the prison together with the convicts. This involves a transference of the personal experiences of the inmates and the structural and customary forms of the criminal groups from the free world into the penitentiary.[10]

It would be impossible to deny the correctness of the "importation" theory. It underestimates, however, the specificity of confinement and the accompanying force of the strivings on the part of the prisoners to reduce their deprivation, a fact which exerts a decisive influence on the form of the organization of prison life. In this study, I present arguments in favor of the "deprivation" hypothesis.

At first glance, one could assume that every resocialization institution creates pain for the incarcerated. In each such institution one should seek those elements which are nonexistent in the others. Their absence or presence should be associated with differences in the degree of deprivation and therefore the divergent pictures of "hidden life."

This was the path I chose to follow in my study when the portraits of the informal structure of the prison community I had made proved to be decidedly different. I sought out those elements specific to the situation in each institution, and every time I could determine another way of solving or alleviating the pain. In this way I attained a different image of the structure.

In this chapter I demonstrate the significance of differences in the economic infrastructure for the informal structure of the inmate community— for the emergence and transformations of the "hidden life" of the prison. In the next two chapters I show that this factor influences the relations between the functionaries and prisoners (chapter 7) and even the relations between the functionaries (chapter 8).

Against the "importation" origin of "hidden life"

How is the domination of the "git people" and "fests" over the remaining prisoners possible considering that it is so easy to turn them into "victims"? It suffices, after all, to dip a cloth into a toilet bowl and, making one's way across the prison, to slap every "git person" with it in order to turn all the "people" into "victims." This is an essential question, and such incidents actually do take place in penal institutions. But what happens then?

Institution A was the scene of the following incident: a prisoner who arrived from another penal institution claimed to be a "git person." In reality he was only a "sucker," but before the "git people" found this out they all had shaken his hand. As a result, all the "people" in this cell block were "victimized." This was an enormous tragedy for them; several of the inmates inflicted injuries on themselves. The prison elite, aware of the perils for the "people" from such accidental forms of "victimization," decided to raise unconditionally to the rank of "people" all the inmates degraded in that fashion.

The same occurs when many "people" are maliciously "mucked"; it is still easier for them to be readmitted to the "git people" than for the other "victims." The perpetrator of this act is usually beaten and even degraded to a "fag." This is both a penalty and a warning addressed to the others. Only those who were raped without reason or those who were "paid out" were "beyond help." It is physically impossible to carry this out on all the "git people." The problem which is deliberated here is actually whether the norms themselves, observed by the "people" and the "fests," contain a threat of the liquidation of those groups (and therefore of the so-called code).

I. Let us imagine a situation in which a group of strangers of the same sex become isolated from society against their own will, deprived of all rights and amenities. Every so often consumer articles are delivered to the place where they are housed, but not enough goods to meet the requirements of all the confined persons. The way in which the goods are divided and the organization of the lives of these people depend on decisions that they make themselves. The group may divide the goods into equal portions corresponding to the number of people and in the same way divide activities which organize its life, so that everyone would carry the same burden. This choice, however, condemns everyone to dissatisfaction and permanent deprivation.

There is yet another way—some of the members of the community appropriate at the cost of the others a sufficient amount of goods to satisfy their own requirements. This model seems to have many elements in common with prison confinement. In prison the distribution of goods and the organization of life are imposed by regulations. A solution to these two problems followed the first of the described paths: each prisoner receives the same amount and performs the same duties. Distribution produces the above mentioned consequence—universal dissatisfaction. It is my contention that the incarcerated reject this solution and strive toward an illegal redistribution of goods and duties. They wish to appropriate goods belonging to others and to burden the others with duties. This type of division leads to an emergence of two distinct social categories: those who appropriate the goods for themselves, and those deprived of the goods.

This method of division generates a social need for its justification. In the face of a lack of objective criteria, upon which basis such a justification would be feasible, justifications founded on the outcome of a mutual perception appear: the exploited and the exploiter. The latter perceives the exploited as deprived of certain attributes of humanity, as a thing, and negates his subjectivity. The exploited, in turn, views the exploiter as a person who enjoys a certain superiority, in the face of which the exploited must withdraw and feel helpless. The justification of exploitation ("I deserve more since I possess certain features, which you do not have") becomes materialized in the form of a normative system which sanctions the division into "people" and "suckers."

The introduction of norms and sanctions leads to their internalization and an identification with a certain role and category of people ("I'm a sucker," "I belong to the suckers," "They say I'm a sucker," "I am a person," "I belong to the people"). The realization of the sanctions becomes possible because of the organization of the exploiters—an integration which creates a social structure on the basis of their interests, the interests of a group. In this way, a dichotomic social structure appears:

"people" and "suckers." A "person" is the master, a "sucker" is the instrument he uses, and a "fag" is a commodity which is consumed (homosexual intercourse).

The quantitative ratio between the exploiters and exploited which guarantees the stability of the configuration depends on the number of goods in a situation when certain duties have to be performed (cleaning the cell, washing the toilet, etc.) as well as on necessary social forces which guarantee the retention of the structure—in other words, an effective functioning of sanctions. The seeming equilibrium is constantly disturbed and is reinstated by regulating the number of members in the given categories. Transference from one prison to another, or an abnormal fluctuation in the number of inmates (released or admitted) can create a more permanent and greater disturbance of those proportions. Let us examine two possible model situations.

The first situation can occur when the decisive majority is composed of "suckers." This situation might signify that the proportions between the number of the "people" and "suckers" have been deranged, with the accompanying existence of a sufficiently organized social force ("people") who guarantee the retention of the structure. A decisively larger number of "suckers" is the reason why the "people" have wider access to the goods and services which the first group can offer. This is why sanctions applied by the "people" for resistance and disobedience on the part of the "suckers" can be mild and used inconsistently. If a "person" does not obtain some article from a "sucker," he is not interested in organizing repression, since he can obtain the article from a number of other "suckers." The competition between "people" for priority in the exploitation of the "suckers" also grows weaker.

This situation might signify not only the derangement of the proportions but also the absence of a social force that guarantees the effective functioning of sanctions. The exploitation of the "suckers" by the "people" is then highly limited or totally impossible. The reason for this state of affairs is an effectively organized protection of the "suckers" or even active struggle with the "people." The "people" as a minority are repressed and even combated by the "suckers." This type of prison is called "suckers' own" by the "people," and they are afraid of being moved there.

As a consequence of the earlier mentioned causes, a situation can occur in which the decisive majority is composed of the "people." The intensive exploitation of the "suckers" which would take place in this case has, however, its objective boundaries. Everything can be extorted, the "suckers'' can be forced to work or used to satisfy sexual needs, but not all the "people" would be capable of exploiting the "suckers" in the same way. Competition emerges between the "people" for priority in this domain as well as exploitation of the "people" by the "people" when the "exploited" becomes a "sucker." This is not in accordance with the accepted principles; we are dealing here with an instrumental treatment of rules. In order to reinstate the equilibrium of the configuration, it becomes necessary to expel part of the "people" who then must increase the ranks of the "suckers." "Affairs are arranged," "mines are laid": A steals cigarettes from B and hides them under C's pillow. B, looking for his belongings, ultimately finds them, and C is regarded as a thief. Since he has violated a rule which says that a "person" cannot steal from another "person," he is expelled from the group and becomes a "sucker." The avalanche-like process of alienating part of the "people" from the group in a way which indicates an instrumental treatment of rules, can lead to a situation in which those rejected by the group will organize in self-defense and will recognize that it was not they who broke the rules but those who expelled them.

It is my conviction that the situation described above took place in institution A where in the past there was a large number of "people", the rest being "suckers" and "fags." Both the new inmates (newly sentenced) and those who were conveyed from other institutions were mainly "people." As the functionaries said, "hidden life flourished." The system of norms was developed and sanctions sharpened. Cultural-educational work with the inmates became impossible. If, for example, a "person" and a "sucker" were told to play chess at the same table in the recreation hall, and the "sucker" leaned on the table, then the latter automatically was contaminated—a "git person" could not touch it or the chess pieces. It was also impossible to organize games: a group of inmates divided into two teams was supposed to play handball. After the first few serves many of them, despite the fact that they stood further to the back of the field, did not participate in the game and even avoided all contact with the ball. It appeared that the ball was touched by a "sucker" who contaminated it—none of the "people" would handle it to avoid becoming a "sucker." If during the morning roll call one of the inmates said "nice weather today," then none of the "people" left for work. The word "nice" is a "curse," and by saying "nice weather" the weather itself was "cursed" and became "unclean"; the "people" could not make contact with the "unclean" weather. If a letter from home contained the expression: "Listen, son, to what I have to say to you,'' then the recipient destroyed it before others could see it since the first letters in the phrase ''I have to say to you'' in Polish form the word ''cunt'' which is also a ''curse.''

The slightest disturbance of norms is enough to be expelled from the ''people.'' The ''suckers'' and ''fags'' were used for even the most menial chores. Some of them had to carry an ashtray from one ''person'' to another in the cell (''constant cruising''), tickle the soles of their feet with a feather, or masturbate them at their beck and call. The ''suckers'' were total slaves, but even they were unable to satisfy all the ''people.'' Conflicts arose among the ''people'' concerning priority in exploiting the ''suckers'' and ''fags''; the ''people'' also began exploiting each other. Often, they expelled someone from the group by ''cursing'' and ''mucking'' without any reason; they ''laid mines'' and accused each other.

The resulting struggle concerned power and leadership in the cell, the cell block, and the whole institution. The feeling of injustice among the prisoners who had been expelled, or were in the process of being expelled, grew. They claimed that they used the principles and rules of the ''code,'' as contrasted with those who ''expel'' without any valid reason. In this way, at a certain stage, the rejected, feeling wronged and hostile toward the ''people'' ''founded a group of fests'': ''we are fest and they are git.'' In other words, both ''are in order.'' The ''fests'' originally constituted a small group of the convicts. They observed the same principles as the ''people,'' although the latter ''did not acknowledge them'' since the ''fests started to cooperate with the 'screws' and are permitted to walk with a key.'' The fact that handling a key did not harm the ''fests'' in their own eyes was particularly incriminating for the ''git people,'' but at the same time it increased the animosity of the ''fests'' toward the ''people.''

The administration used the fact that a group hostile toward the ''git people'' and favorably inclined toward the staff came into being. All the jobs traditionally held by prisoners were entrusted to the ''fests,'' whose animosity toward the ''people'' was further stirred. The results came soon: a ''fest'' who worked as an orderly, a helper of the guard, used to carry keys to the cells. He opened the cells occupied mainly by the ''fests,'' let them out into the corridor, and proceeded to cells dominated by the ''people.'' The ''fests,'' who had the advantage of greater numbers, entered the cells of the ''people'' and beat up the occupants until they renounced the ''code''—in other words, until they ceased to be ''people'' or joined the ''fests.'' The more obstinate ones were ''mucked'' and ''turned into victims.''

The "fests" also took control over the newcomers to the institution. The number of members in their group increased considerably. The fact that the "fests" used force to degrade the "people," together with a situation in which the administration chose to ignore the entire event (everything took place in full sight of the personnel), forced the "git people" to break the rule forbidding them to file complaints. Such a motion could now incriminate the "fests" or functionaries of the prison staff with certain dire consequences. The administration was compelled to limit the unhampered degradation of the "git people" by the "fests" since a complaint filed to a court is proof of the administration's poor performance. The "fests" also limited the application of "degrading by force" which could threaten them with a court case. But at the same time, they boasted to the "git people" that they still kept the rule about not filing charges.

In their struggle against the "git people," the "fests" began to use other methods concerning relations between the groups. As a result, the "people," deprived of their members, decided to abandon still another rule which said that once expelled from the group, the given "person" could not be readmitted. There would be no "setting straight," no "returning to the rank of a person." Originally, the inmate (a former "person") who was victimized and wished to be "straightened out" had to make his way to institution Z, where the prisoners were older and with longer prison histories. It was maintained that only the local leader of the "people" had the right to "set straight." Institution Z also had a prison hospital, and in order to get there, prisoners had to perform self-mutilations ("slash themselves," "swallow something," "dust their eyes with something"). The head of the "people" in institution Z (or another important "git person") became acquainted, directly or via intermediaries, with the case and made a decision. The whole affair came down to a suitable payment for the person who "set straight" and made it possible for the "victimized" prisoner to return to institution A as a "person." This procedure lasted for quite some time, until the leaders of the "git people" in institution A decided that the profits should no longer go to institution Z. After all, they reasoned, they too were "people" and were even better acquainted with the case. Putting a stop to the travel to institution Z to be "set straight" would settle many problems.

In this situation, inmates alienated from the "people" organized a group of "fests" who, as we remember, are hostile to the "people." The "fests" cooperated with the administration; in return, they received all sorts of profitable job assignments, which offered them the opportunity to obtain various articles by means other than the exploitation of the "victims" (as is done by the "git people"). This arrangement grew increasingly stable. Neither the "fests" nor the "git people" introduced an "America" (a test for novices), which was supposed to recommend their particular group. Nonetheless, the secret period of testing and exploiting the new inmates was retained by both groups.

II. Let us imagine the following situation: the "people" are confined, but possibilities exist for emolument by means other than exploitation. The raw material and tools available in the prison workshops create the opportunity for illegal production and trade. The inmates can receive products and money for the articles sold. This procedure calls for cooperation and a division of profits. The interpersonal relations, therefore, cannot be similar to those in the above outlined models. If inmate A wants to produce something from a piece of metal, then he needs several machines manned by other prisoners. The production of an additional element is connected with the necessity of coming to an understanding and sharing the profit in return for sharing the work and the risk.

If this situation involves a "git person" then we might ask whether the production of that element would be possible if the "person" behaved toward a "sucker" in accordance with principles described in the earlier models. The answer is obviously no. The "sucker" can be forced to do many things but one cannot have him risk punishment for illicit production. The threat of a sanction does not motivate him to embark on this sort of activity (he may even refuse), and scrutiny itself can impede the process of illegal production. He must be encouraged to become engaged in the production, to want to do this work in secret, and to become involved. Therefore, the "person" must alter his attitude toward the "sucker" in order to establish such a partnership and secure his participation in the profit, which would mean the obliteration of social differences. One needs the other, if they wish to produce and earn.

A social structure based on cooperation emerges in which one can distinguish a certain category of people from the point of view of functions filled in production and barter. A characteristic trait of this model is the domination of external sources of illicit income, which was decidedly greater in institution B than in institution A. The use of external sources in institution B is no longer a function of belonging to the "people," the "suckers," or the "fags" and, therefore, their nature is also different than it is in institution A.

III. Let's consider a third situation, that of a penal institution in which the inmates work outside the prison for a certain period of time and are employed by local production enterprises. The possibility of coming to a tacit understanding with the workers of those institutions makes it possible for the inmates to obtain desired "commodities" in a different way than the exploitation of or cooperation with other convicts. The consumption of these articles is also feasible outside the penal institution.

The social structure of the inmates is based on close liaisons established in the place of work and cells ("tea drinkers") or on the basis of territorial origin ("countrymen"). In this situation, the existence of a group of "people" appears to arise due to the transition of certain traditions from closed penal institutions. Nonetheless, the social position of the "people" does not seem to be higher than that of the rest of the inmates who do not belong to the "people." Those two communities live alongside each other. The "people" isolate themselves against the other prisoners primarily in the institution. Outside, when they work together with the "non-code users," they often begin to cooperate in order to earn supplementary income. On the basis of this cooperation, permanent, friendly relations appear, but they occur mainly outside the prison, "not before the eyes of the people." Conflicts based on the appropriation of someone else's goods do not arise in this community. Everyone, with some effort, can win the goods independently, without any help, and not at the cost of the other inmates.

The typical feature of this model is the distinctly external type of sources of illegal income (the internal type occurs only to a slight extent), mainly as a result of gaining and consuming the goods outside the penal institution.

The shape of the prison social structure and its functions are conditioned by access to consumer goods and the level of cooperation or exploitation in obtaining them. These two variables determine the type of institution (closed, semi-open) and more rarely, the type of production enterprises in which the inmates are employed (mainly in the closed penal institutions).

If the raw material used by the enterprise is unattractive as a market commodity and the tools are not useful for eventual illegal production, then the manner of obtaining these goods will be like one of the situations described in the first model. For example, in an enterprise that produces elements of reinforced concrete weighing up to twenty tons and uses such basic tools as spades, picks, axes, and cranes, it is impossible to barter or sell (without great risk), and nothing else can be produced here.

One must conclude, therefore, that the basic function of the structure of the prison community is the illegal gaining and distribution of consumer goods. The nature of the structure is determined by the way the goods are obtained and their access. The type of penal institution and the production tasks of the enterprises in those institutions define the range of access to those goods and the way of obtaining them. Of course, another important factor is the professional skills and qualifications of the inmates. If someone does not know how to use the tools or has no manual ability, then he will not be able to produce articles for sale. As a rule, the young inmates cannot handle complicated tools and thus embark on illicit production to a lesser degree than their older colleagues.

If prison authorities were to introduce changes into the economic organization of the penal institution in a way that defines the range and ways of obtaining consumer goods, then the prisoners would strive toward entering into such interpersonal relations which would make it possible to gain optimum profits in the new situation. They would also retain certain old patterns of interaction as long as the latter remain functional. This seems to explain why in different penal institutions we can come across both similar and different elements within the existing informal structures of the prison community.

7.

Between the "Screws" and the "Crooks"

Variants of the Relations between the Prisoners and the Staff:
Hostility, Symbiosis, Parallelism

It is often stressed that the informal organization of the inmates is directed against the formal goals or organizational units of the prison—the school, the workplace, the administration, the regulations, and so forth. This attitude is typical for the adherents of the deprivation theory of the origins of "hidden life."[1] The existence of the prison subculture, if not outright blocking the process of resocialization, makes it difficult, while the prison administration, established for its realization, encounters the animosity of the inmates. This animosity is manifested predominantly by the most hardened adherents and leaders of "hidden life." Rioting is the most acute form of prisoners' hostility toward functionaries.[2] Hostility is, on the one hand, evoked by frustration caused by the pains of confinement and the representatives of the prison system.[3] On the other hand, it is a defensive expression against functionaries' aggression.

Without ignoring the hostile attitudes of the inmates toward the staff, it is emphasized that a tacit agreement appears between the leaders of the "hidden life" and the prison personnel.[4] The authority enjoyed by the leaders of the "hidden life" is possible only with the silent support of the prison employees. The model of the social functioning of the inmates established by the leading group guarantees the maintenance of a certain cohesion and order within the community. Distinct forms of decisive disobedience of the prisoners are stifled by the ruling group. The administration, therefore, has secured a certain minimum of order in the prison, the price being the recognition of the "rights" of those who rule the community. If, however, the administration were to abolish those "rights" which remain at odds with the regulations, then the existing order and stability would cease, and the resultant state of anarchy could lead to a riot.

One can say that the community of the prisoners and the functionaries is capable of arranging a coexistence based on joint benefit. These benefits can be generated not only by mutual nonintervention but also by cooperation of a material nature. The contraband food, cigarettes, alcohol, or narcotics involves both the inmate and the functionaries.[5] The symbiotic links between the staff and the prisoners can come down to profits from mutual nonintervention and cooperation in obtaining personal gains (not only material ones, for example, better treatment).

The supporters of the "importation" theory of the origin of "hidden life" see the relation of the inmates to the functionaries in still another way. The informal organization of the prisoners realizes aims similar to those of the criminal groups outside prison, but as a result of the limited opportunities for committing crimes, it concentrates on the exchange of experiences, the making of new contacts, and the perfection of criminal skills.[6] Because of these goals, the incarcerated try to conceal their activity from the administration. This is not an antagonistic or symbiotic relationship of the prisoners and the administration, but rather a social parallelism of functioning.

In this chapter I try to show three phases of shaping relations between the prisoners and the functionaries in organizationally different prison conditions, and the ultimate effect typical for those conditions this process accomplishes.

The Second Authority in Prison:
The "Screws" versus the "Crooks"

The informal structure of the prison community in institution A delineates a picture of the relationship between particular categories of prisoners and functionaries. The essence of those relationships can be understood better if one follows some of the changes which occurred not only in institution A, in the relationship: functionaries-prisoners.[7] In the past, the social structure of the inmates in institution A was of a dichotomic nature. The prison staff both in institution A and in other centers assesses the phenomena inherent in "hidden life" as decisively negative.[8] "From the point of view of influence upon the process of resocialization," wrote three high ranking functionaries of the prison system, " 'hidden life' is placed on a scale starting from socially accepted forms (e.g., help in studying), through bypassing regulation orders and prohibitions, up to an informal organization with a criminal ideology, which disorganizes resocialization work in the penitentiary institution."[9] Particular condemnation was expressed for "code users." As one of the functionaries stated, "The code constitutes an extremely dangerous 'ideology,' directed primarily against order, security, discipline, the premises of penitentiary policy, and finally, our social existence. The threat consists of the fact that the 'code users' pass on their attitudes, and contaminate others."[10]

Self-liquidation under coercion, or "elimination of the code by force"

Such an estimate of "hidden life" unambiguously gave rise to the necessity of overcoming it. The problem was which methods to use, "whether one should wage a battle with the criminal subculture by means of a direct attack and reveal the premise of its being combated, or whether the criminal subculture should be eliminated from the life of informal youth groups by enforcing the principles or regulations for imprisonment which include a prohibition of informal groups and the antisocial behavior which is advocated by the 'code.' I believe that the frontal attack against the leaders of 'hidden life' or whole informal groups, which cultivate elements of a criminal subculture extremely dangerous for the course of resocialization, can sometimes be necessary because of the threat to the other convicts on the part of the 'code' and its strong domination among the youth. A direct attack can be a point of departure for a broadly outlined and systematic resocialization."[11]

In institution A, and, as the cited material suggests, in other prisons as well, this "direct attack" consisted of breaking up "hidden life" by force. The accepted method was the result of a conviction that "hidden life" is not the product of the prison—it is not caused by the prison—and therefore should be attacked and destroyed. Initially this was done by applying the very principles of "hidden life."

A "git person" asked whether he is a "code user" cannot deny the fact. Otherwise, he automatically becomes a "sucker," particularly if he is overheard by other "people" and no longer can return to his group. The administration decided to capitalize on this. After new prisoners were admitted to the institution they were asked about their membership in the "code users." Those who denied affiliation were led out of the room, and the others were beaten by guards armed with truncheons until they publicly renounced the "code," automatically turning themselves into "suckers." This method became known among the "git people" as "elimination of the code by force." Despite the brutal measures, many of the inmates did not waver, although their ranks became considerably reduced. This method soon became universally recognized in penitentiaries, and "code users" transferred to other institutions were well aware of the "welcome" which awaited them.

After a certain time, whenever the selected "code users" were left alone with the guards, they cut their own wrists on smashed window glass, turned on the attacking guards and, "pumped blood" by rhythmically opening and closing their fists.

Originally, this method of defending "humanity" was effective, and the staff retreated. But when this situation repeated itself regularly, the guards came to the conclusion that the inmates would never stop using it, and not only in those particular circumstances. The prison staff therefore returned to the "elimination of the code by force" despite the "pumping." Once again, their methods brought results, and after some time the inmates universally answered "no" to the question, "Are you a code user?" Did this mean the elimination of the "code"? Not in the least. It soon became evident that the "code users" simply changed the term "code user" into "one who uses the code." Therefore, no one was a "code user" (unless he was an uninitiated inmate who tried to alter his position in "hidden life," i.e., a "sucker"), but there were many of those who "used the code."

In the meantime, the "people" also abolished the prohibition of readmitting the "suckers" to the "git people." The state of being a "sucker" was annulled mainly for those who were "deprived of the code by force." They also abandoned the principle of not filing complaints. "People" had believed that official law and its institutions should not be utilized, but in the face of brutal treatment contrary to the law, they departed from that principle.

An example of the struggle waged against the "git people" using the internal principles binding for its members is also seen in the statement made by one of the directors of a penal institution: "It follows that the 'people' usually constitute from 30 to 40 percent of all the convicts. In the Correctional Institution in Malbork we have as many as 80 to 90 percent . . . for our institution, 1967-1972 was a period of errors and failures in a struggle against the 'git people.' There was often a confrontation of force. This began in 1967 with a riot among members of the brass band. The 'people' did not want to play on 'suckered' instruments. In other situations the best students in the prison school got worse grades because the 'people' forbade them to study. There were also strikes in the workshops, lasting for several minutes. We had two cases when the leaders of the 'code' were punished with solitary confinement—the 'people' protested by refusing to work. When a 'sucker' helped one of the drivers carry bread into the kitchen, the 'people' decided that the bread was 'unclean' and refused to eat it. . . . The 'people' demanded that they be issued their own mugs, plates, and bowls because a 'person' should not eat from dishes used by a 'sucker.' Three times the guards were attacked with the intention of stealing keys and escape. One such case involved a severe beating and the second one ended with the death of our worker. . . . Our counter-actions had . . . little effect. We created separate groups for the weaker inmates to protect them and accepted the resultant division. But contact at school and in the workshops continued, where the 'non-code users' were insulted and attacked. We decided to retaliate: the prosecutor intervened twice and arrested those who resorted to violence. . . . We also began to use their own weapons. In 1968 we had in our institution the greatest ideo-logue of the 'code,' known as 'Hunchback,' who played the role of the oracle and decided who and for what offense an inmate should be 'dropped down'—'suckered.' He also collected information about each of the in-mates. If a letter of an inmate transferred from another institution made a critical remark about one of the 'people,' then this ruthless pathological case 'suckered' everyone. He originally came to our institution from Poznan. Using an opportunity when one of our staff members went to Poznan, I wrote a note to one of our inmates who corresponded with a friend from the Poznan Correctional Institution: 'Beware of the Hunch-back—signed: the People.' This note was sent from Poznan, and its effect was immediate. This powerful 'git person,' highest in the hierarchy, sud-denly became a nobody. We regarded this method of fighting as unethical and were simply testing how ruthless the laws observed by the 'code' are. After a tragic incident in 1968 we received security forces from the Penal Institution in Sztum. This was a source of new strength and energy; we felt safer and stronger."[12]

Fighting against the criminal subculture by direct attack and the disclo-sure of the very premises of this fight[13] was an attempt to defeat the "code" with its own weapons. It showed that although it is feasible to correct the most dangerous symptoms of this phenomenon, it still remains impossible to liquidate it. The apparently rigid principles of "hidden life" can be made flexible or simply altered. The phenomenon of "hidden life" continues to exist and appears as a phantom which changes places and appearances. These experiences, moreover, made the administration aware of the fact that the struggle waged against "hidden life" actually favors its development.

"The official division of the convicts into the 'code users' and the 'non-code users' leads to an integration of the groups of the inmates, and their existence. Moreover, it is dangerous for the administration of the institution to openly support one of these groups. Disturbing the equilibrium between them can lead to menacing incidents and, furthermore, it fails to bring the phenomenon under control since in the place of the group or elite being confronted a new one appears."[14]

The ineffectiveness of apartheid

The next method of combating "hidden life" was preceded by a greater dose of reflection. The administration accepted the "transmission" theory of the origin of "hidden life" and realized that it should be possible to eradicate the "hidden life" introduced into the prison, and that its premises could be proven to be an irrational and unnecessary game. That this did not happen probably had something to do with the prison. But this was just one step toward analyzing the causes of "hidden life" and the essence of failure of the methods used thus far to combat it.

It was recognized that the specific feature of the "hidden life" is a division into a group of dominating prisoners and those who are totally exploited by them. If so, it should have been sufficient to separate the two groups and prevent contact for "hidden life" to lose its foundation and fall apart. Attempts were made to do precisely that.

In institution A it was decided to place the "code users" in a cell all by themselves and the "suckers" together with the "suckers." The new arrivals were asked which group they belonged to earlier and then directed to appropriate cells. This method, however, was abandoned for two reasons:

1. Many of the "suckers" claimed to be "code users" and the latter quickly became aware of the newcomers' true status. Such a "sucker" was constantly exploited. He was often harassed and raped. He was also told that he would be killed if he were to complain to the administration. Therefore, the administration usually found out about such an inmate only when he finally broke down and attempted to commit suicide or when distinct signs of bodily assault became apparent (bruised and cut face, blood

coming out of the shoes of a prisoner who was forced to "ride a bicycle" in the night, etc.).

2. This method not only failed to contribute to the liquidation of "hidden life," it did not even limit its negative symptoms. In the cells originally filled exclusively with "code users," some of them were, after a certain time, turned into "suckers," while in cells with the "suckers" a division into those who were worse and better appeared, which in effect was identical to the division into "people" and "suckers."

Experiments conducted in institution A ended with the same negative results in other institutions as well: "It often happens that the so-called degraded [in 'hidden life'] convicts are morally no higher than the 'git people.' From practice I know that if for their own good the weaker inmates are concentrated in one cell, the same negative phenomena appear in it, often in a more sophisticated and dangerous form. Hence, I propose that not distinguishing the victims is just as purposeful as eliminating the leaders."[15]

This statement can be supported with still another: "It seemed that we had committed many mistakes in combating the negative form of 'hidden life.' These errors include the separate confinement of 'code users' and 'non-code users,' as well as the so-called victims. Based on many years of practice, we became convinced that such separate confinement leads to the intensification of the negative forms of 'hidden life.' "[16]

Divide et impera

If the absence of positive results of the first method of combating "hidden life" seems to undermine the theory of its "external" origin—the introduction and reproduction in prison of the criminal subculture—then the ineffectiveness of the second variety proves that the origin of divisions within "hidden life" should not be connected with the personality of the prisoner, that is domination and subservience. Neither one nor the other, introduced into the prison, is the cause. These experiments predominantly show the irrefutable tendency for its existence and rebirth in all circumstances.

The failures suffered by the prison staff in their battle with "hidden life" convinced them that "it is impossible to liquidate it."[17] They became more open to arguments proposed by the supporters of the deprivation theory.[18] Nonetheless, they made no headway in this respect other than to accept the existence of "hidden life," and the only thing which could be done, in their opinion, was to prevent its most drastic symptoms. The main emphasis was put on prevention.

The development of a broadly conceived propaganda campaign was proposed using broadcasts on the institutional radio network, conferences, meetings, discussions, and individual conversation with the inmates in order to "make the convicts aware of the fact that the negative symptoms of 'hidden life' are harmful, that they result not only in disciplinary punishment but also in harsher verdicts. To this end sentences must be skillfully passed for crimes committed while in detention or in the institution. . . . Disapproval expressed by the prison administration for the behavior of people strongly connected with the criminal subculture, especially the leaders of 'hidden life,' should, above all, ridicule their infantile behavior, unsuitable for a mature person."[19]

It was acknowledged that "the essential element of restricting 'hidden life' is the proper use of data about the degree of demoralization among the convicts, their return to crime, and susceptibility to resocialization, both while classifying and placing the convicts and while dividing them into school, didactic, or work groups. . . . By stratifying the environment of the inmates with the help of this criterion, which is fully supported by the rules in force, one should take into account primarily the needs and possibilities of such a programming of penitentiary steps as to make it possible to manipulate, in a purposeful and flexible way, the emerging informal groups in the penal institution."[20]

"An operation of capital significance for the limitation of 'hidden life' was, beginning with 1969, the confinement of juveniles together with suitably chosen and well behaved adult first offenders. The possibility of confining juveniles together with adults sentenced for anti-state crimes, murder or rape, was excluded."[21]

It was emphasized that a factor of particular importance in "preventing the symptoms of 'hidden life' is also the matter of a suitably extensive involvement of juvenile convicts in vocational training and production. These are factors which indubitably distract the inmates from participating in the so-called 'hidden life,' since they result in physical and mental exhaustion. An extremely relevant factor which prevents 'hidden life' is appropriate use of the convicts' leisure time."[22] The cooperation of the administration of the penal institutions with parents is also important.[23]

All the methods of counteracting "hidden life" were applied in institution A: anti-"code" propaganda, the stratification of the convicts, and confinement of adults together with juveniles, work, studying, and contacts with the family. It is difficult to estimate their actual destructive impact on "hidden life." The phenomenon still exists and nothing seems to forecast its disappearance. Neither does it seem that the assumed novelty of introducing adult offenders into institutions for juveniles was of such capital importance. In institution A the adult inmates belong either to the "fests," the "people," or the "Swiss."

"Formerly, twenty-one was some sort of magical age beyond which the juveniles ceased to be connected with a criminal group and could become normal convicts. This has changed now, and the age of the inmates does not play as great a role. An inmate who is older than twenty-one becomes a 'fogey who's OK,' or a 'fogey with the heart of a minor.' "[24.]

Strict control of the prison community by the staff appears to be much more effective for the prevention of the negative symptoms of "hidden life." "Both of the directors of the Central Administration of Penal Institutions who held this post in the 1970s . . . first of all increased the emphasis on the so-called operational work which was directly connected with expanding the range of the prisoners' unproductive work of a discretionary nature."[25]

"It became apparent that . . . penitentiary penetration led to systematic changes of the forms of 'hidden life' and to systematic elimination of its most dangerous forms. Our experiences have shown that convicts organized in informal groups, if aware of the fact that we are familiar with the problem of prison subculture and react to the symptoms of that subculture, must abandon the most drastic forms . . . although we . . . realize that we do not eliminate 'hidden life' in the penal institution in its entirety."[26]

Thanks to this "penetration," it was possible to rapidly extract and "separate the leaders from the environment which created them. Their confinement among adult first offenders with another mentality became a very effective way of breaking up the informal groups of the convicts, especially the 'code users.' " This also gave positive results in work with the leaders themselves. The guidelines of the Director of the Central Administration of Penal Institutions, issued on June 30, 1972, allowed the confinement of juvenile convicts who were noted for their bad conduct and who acted as "organizers of 'hidden life' together with adult first offenders in penal institutions in Strzelce Opolskie and Brzeg. These guidelines were in direct opposition to the practice at that time and proved to be one of the essential steps toward solving the problem of interest to us."[27]

"The question still remains of utilizing gaps in the 'hidden life' or the creation of such objective situations in which the supporters of the 'code' must choose between the values of a criminal subculture and others. I shall give an example of one such undertaking. It was decided that the juveniles would take meals according to work groups and not at an arbitrarily chosen time and place at the table, as before. In the new situation there was no possibility to sit down according to the criteria of the "code" and the only possibility remaining was to resign from the meal. Decisions made on the basis of choosing certain values meant that it could be seen which value is greater—the meal or the observance of the principles of the criminal subculture. There are more examples of similar methods."[28]

In the Correctional Institution in Malbork it was decided to treat the "code" as "vulgar." "Even if a single word in a letter was written using the 'code,' the inmate was prohibited from sending or receiving such correspondence. He was informed of the reason. . . . During the morning roll call the inmates were lined up according to height; before this, the 'people' stood in front, followed by the 'suckers' at some distance from the rest."[29]

In one of the institutions, "nonadmittance of 'code users' to production, additional encouragement to take part in cultural-educational activities, and allowing participation dependent on whether the inmate 'used the code' were reasons why the 'code' began to break down."[30]

A positive attitude "can bring apparent concessions in favor of the inmates, for example, the dismissal of the so-called 'fags' from serving meals. I see no point in fighting those inmates who demand that the 'fags' be discharged. We have the technical means to always win these battles, but we won't alter the consciousness of the convicts, and an open confrontation will only contribute to the integration of the inmate community."[31]

An analysis of the experiments conducted by the prison staff with "hidden life" paved the way for special "directives for counterposing and overcoming the negative symptoms of prison subculture,"[32] which employ any of the methods presented here. The "Directives" recognized the symptoms of "hidden life" as:

a. in the cell—carrying out cleaning chores [by the exploited inmates], change of beds and restrictions on communal use of the table, separate storage of dishes, change of clothes, keeping to the side or pushing aside an inmate when a superior enters the cell, the imposition of menial jobs, admitting to all the misconduct committed in the cell, or accusation on the part one of the residents of the cell as the guilty party, the refusal to go for exercise or to the washroom;

b. during the exercise period—attempts at illegal communication, forming in groups, exclusion from joining groups, impeding contact with functionaries;

c. in the washroom—forcing help in washing, signs of bodily assault, new tattoos;

d. at place of work—hindering work, extortion of product parts, prevention of raising labor output, breaking machines;

e. in school—provocative behavior toward the teacher, malicious interference in conducting lessons, preventing classmates from profiting from the lessons, preventing personal contact with the teacher during recess, etc.[33]

In institution A, the prison staff controls the inmate community mainly by means of a careful selection of the make-up of the cells. This is to assure that none of the groups would win decisive superiority in the cell. Furthermore, in every cell, workplace, and school the functionaries have their own informants among the "people," the "fests," the "Swiss," and the "victims."[34]

The safest form of contact between the informers and the staff are periodic talks with prisoners. All the inmates of a given cell are summoned in turn to such an interview with the counselor. Each is asked whether he has any complaints or matters to be settled. Of course, one of the inmates is an informer who reports in detail about the events in the cell over a given period of time.

The contact between the "informer" and the functionaries can also take place on other occasions (for example, in emergency cases), but it is dangerous. Physical contact with a functionary is very suspicious and can become a pretext for accusations of "denouncing" and for expulsion from the group. This is sometimes exploited by the functionaries; for example, by approaching prisoners standing alone, or by summoning one of them for a talk, the staff can arouse the suspicion of the remaining inmates.

The staff pays special attention to controlling the "git people." In this case, but not only, the functionaries also try to influence the situation within the group. Through informers they decide what steps are to be taken by the group. They instruct them, for example, to "victimize" a "git person" who disrupts order in the prison. They also influence the choice of leaders of the "code users" in cells, in cell blocks, and in the whole institution. Inconvenient candidates or leaders already chosen are "dropped down" by the functionaries who order their informants to "muck" them.

Two or three years before my arrival in institution A, the leader of the "people" was discharged. The "code users" secretly elected a successor, but the administration quickly established his identity. Everything seemed to indicate that the new leader would become a source of unrest. The administration feared disturbances and an intensification of "hidden life." It therefore instructed the "victims" to "drop him down" and consequently a new leader was chosen. The situation, however, was repeated, and he too became "victimized." The atmosphere in the institution grew tense. Finally, the warden proposed meeting a group representing the "git people" and a joint appointment of the "head" of the "people." The "code users" agreed and in this way both sides accepted the newly chosen leader.

But the administration also makes concessions to the "people." It does not react, for instance, to the custom of forbidding the "victims" to sit at the table and eat with the "code users." To a certain extent it also tolerates the exploitation of the "victims" by the "code users." Moreover, it does not employ the "victims" and "fags" in the laundry, the kitchen, and for serving meals—these functions are performed by the "fests."

This situation demands of the staff a more thorough familiarity with the positions held by the prisoners in "hidden life." Neglect and permission for the "victim" to serve meals can result in a hunger strike by the "code users." It is difficult for the administration to subsequently discharge such an inmate because this would be tantamount to public recognition of the rights of "hidden life."

Such an error committed in the recent past caused the administration considerable trouble. The "git people" refused to eat, demanding that the "victim" who served meals in the wards be discharged. The administration refused to meet the request. The hunger strike lasted for over a week, and it appeared that the "git people" had no plans to stop. When hunger became intolerable, however, they were at a loss what to do. First they tried to send an illicit message to juvenile recidivists in another prison where the local "people" were regarded as an oracle in matters connected with the "code" and could offer sensible advice. The message, however, fell into the hands of the administration of institution A. Usually, in instances of attempted illicit contact with anyone outside the institution, the administration tries to establish the inmate's identity and penalize him, but this time it was decided to break from procedure. The functionaries themselves wrote an answer and, using their own channels, forwarded this supposed reply to the striking inmates. The "people" read that in such cases as their own, the food should be placed on a table or by an open window. If possible, the door of the cell should be left open and then the "unclean qualities" would be "aired out." Thus the hunger strike ended and some time later, the administration ceased to employ "victims."

The administration of institution A officially tries to treat all the inmates in the same way, regardless of the group to which they belong—any manipulations remain behind-the-scene. The exception includes the division of functions needed for organizing life in prison: the recreation hall attendants, librarians, barbers, employees of the radio network, corridor orderlies, workers in the laundry and the washrooms. These are "fests" and the "Swiss" whom the administration trusts the most.

The prison staff takes care to set the groups and the inmates within the groups against each other and carries this out with the help of informers. Conflicts between the groups or individual inmates are less of a problem than eventual tacit understandings between the groups or individuals, or the domination of a single group in the institution, a cell block, or a cell; this could become the source of what the functionaries call "the negative symptoms of prison subculture": fights, self-mutilations, a boycott of school, disobedience and aggression toward the staff, riots.

Control and concern for the maintenance of a social equilibrium in the prison does not in the least mean that the administration no longer employs old methods of combating "hidden life." Sometimes the guards will place the hand of a "git person" who causes disturbances into a toilet bowl in order to turn him into a "victim." Thanks to the interception of messages and information provided by the "denouncers," the personnel discovers which of the prisoners smuggled money; it is then taken away during a search. If the guards come across a package containing contraband, they appropriate it and throw the package into the toilet, knowing very well that a "git person" will not touch it because it has become "unclean."

At other times, functionaries resort to physical force. Neither do inmates remain passive—a prisoner who has been "deprived of the code" can "slash himself," and the reasons for this act become universally known. The functionary who used physical force can expect revenge.

One of the counselors, called Jinks, admitted that he insulted the prisoners and "liked to hit." An inmate who reported to him with a personal matter to be settled usually found Jinks lolling in an armchair with his legs on the desk. This was the case until one day an inmate appeared there who refused to stand at attention. He wore an open shirt and glared at the counselor with hands on his hips. Growing furious, Jinks asked through clenched teeth what the problem was, ready to stand up and "slug the crook." The answer—"A hundred dicks"—was more than he could tolerate, but he noticed that the supervising guard was signaling him that about twenty other inmates were waiting outside the door.

Jinks, a well-built man himself, sat down again and although he still "boiled with rage" waited for a further development of the situation. The inmate, who noticed that Jinks had not behaved as usual, struck the glass wall of a 200-liter aquarium with his elbow. Broken glass, water, and fish fell to the floor, but Jinks still did not react. The prisoner backed out of the room and left with the whole group of prisoners waiting for him.

An examination of the circumstances of this incident revealed that the inmates wanted to provoke Jinks. The group waiting behind the door was supposed to come to the inmate's aid, using this opportunity to assault the counselor. "Ever since then" said Jinks, "I don't slug the crooks anymore."

The attitude of the administration to the "fests" is of a dual nature. The profits enjoyed by the administration are unquestionable, but the "fests" have their own principles and do not go too far in their cooperation. They serve as informers, but only as long as it does not harm their own group—hence they are not entirely trusted. Sometimes the informers are capable of passing false information in order to use the administration for settling accounts with other inmates.

The staff also know that the "fests" exploit their functions for material profit, thanks to certain members of the staff. Nonetheless, the staff must pretend to be oblivious to this fact if they wish to have the "fests" on their side and against the "git people"; by permitting this kind of situation the functionaries uphold the attractiveness of the trusties among the prisoners.

All the groups share an animosity toward the "screws" either because they harass them, or, as in the case of the "victims," the "fags," and the "Swiss," because they do not provide sufficient protection against the "code users" or even the "fests," while the "git people" and the "fests" complain that the functionaries protect only the first three groups.

The "fests" do not like the "screws" because they are unable to get rid of the "grubbers"; the "git people" do not like the "screws" because they harass them and let the "fests" fight them. The "Swiss" claim that the "screws" support the "fests" and not them, and the "victims" complain that, just as the "git people," the "screws" regard them as nobodies. Possibly only the "fags" would hold no grudge if not for the fact that the functionaries despise them, as do all the inmates.

The self-destructive hero

A convict's entire life is passed in one and the same place. In all the phases of daily life, he is in direct proximity with a large number of other inmates. Almost every activity is carried out in someone else's view. An inmate has no opportunity to free himself from the others, unless he is punished by solitary confinement, but even here he can be observed by a functionary.

In the cell, the convict performs his bodily functions, eats, washes, undresses and dresses, reads, writes letters, masturbates, cries, and even steals in full sight of the other inmates. He learns and works together with the others, he talks to his family in the presence of functionaries, his letters can be read by the prison staff, and his diary taken during a search. This is why the presence of other people is experienced as a burden of confinement and produces an animosity toward other people.[35]

In institution A, overcrowding is common. The cells have beds (mainly bunks), lockers, a toilet, and, of course, the inmates themselves. There is a shortage of beds, so a mattress placed on the floor under or next to a bed is used as a substitute. Even in such a small place as the cell there are better or worse places to sleep: the bed standing further from the toilet bowl, in winter the bed further from the window and in the summer the one by the window; some prefer to sleep on the highest bunks, others on the lower. It is always better to sleep on a bed than on the floor. A struggle is waged for the preferred places and this gives rise to conflicts.

The outcomes of overcrowding also include other conflicts: prisoners continuously brush against each other and have to wait until the toilet is free. Not all the inmates are able to eat at the same time because there is not enough room at the table. They clean up after the others if it is their turn. They cannot read a book because someone else has borrowed it. Some want to listen to the radio while others do not. Conversations held at night might be disturbing, and so forth.

The inmates' activity is strictly planned around the clock. So much the worse for the prisoner if he is unable to say why and for what purpose he is to be found in a given place, and if he does answer, the justification of the time, place, and activity can only be the day's schedule, regulations, or an eventual order issued by a functionary. A definite schedule defines tasks for whole groups of inmates: pupils to school, workers to the work-shops, the sick to the doctor, meals served at a given time for everyone, the counselor's office hours are the same for everyone, and so forth. Prisoners depart for work and return in closed formations. The movement of the prisoners in the penal institution is controlled by the staff.

It is not always possible to order a large group of prisoners to engage in the same activity in a given place and at a given time. Not everyone can play table tennis because there are not enough tables. Not everyone can eat at the same time—they must wait until there is a place for them. Not everyone can wash and shave at the same time—they must wait until a sink is free. Not all can see the counselor—waiting in a line is a common occurrence.

All of the elements of the organization of the inmates' life mentioned above contribute to an animosity by the inmates toward other people. A competition emerges for priority in settling one's own affairs and for the most favorable position in any given situation. This state of affairs in turn produces conflicts between the prisoners, and their resolution is achieved by forcing concessions. The best chances belong to the persistent individuals, ready to use all possible means in order to attain their goals.

The conflict usually begins with arguments, but they are quickly exhausted by the obstinacy of the two sides. Soon name calling stirs up emotions and makes a solution even more remote. Other measures are employed at this point: someone hits someone else who strikes back, beginning a fight in which one side decides to use a heavy instrument and renders the opponent harmless. Thus the victor sets into motion certain administrative repercussions, faces penal sanctions, and is totally unable to prevent this from happening. Nonetheless, in the eyes of the other inmates he has made his mark as an unyielding man, ready to go further than anyone else could afford to. He is prepared to commit a deed which could result in the strictest legal sanctions.

The boundary of these achievements is therefore the bringing about of such a state of affairs in which that which happens no longer depends on the offender. He is unable to alter the existing situation. An inquiry will be held against him, and others will decide what will happen to him. But this being at the mercy of a situation in which one loses the possibility of influencing one's own fate—"my fate lies in the hands of others and I am unable to alter it"—is recognized by the prisoners' community as an heroic act of courage.

A particular act of courage is to inflict injuries on oneself or to reduce the body to a state in which all control is lost. Even though this could lead to death, "I am not afraid of death, I challenge death—let it take me." Playing with death is connected with gravest danger. The manifestation of complete irresponsibility for one's fate, activity directed against oneself, serves to demonstrate a readiness for anything. Usually these are the sort of people to whom one concedes.

A special case, recognized by the prisoners themselves as abnormal, is the "crazy." This is a person who in his conduct does not follow any rules of behavior and is ready to commit every possible deed regardless of the consequences. He behaves like someone "cut down from the gallows." The "crazy" is kept at a distance, since his conduct is always unpredictable.

The behavior described above forces the administration to assume a special attitude toward the prisoners. In the penal institution, as I have mentioned, the individual is deprived of all self-responsibility which is replaced by the responsibility of the institution for him.[36] After being admitted to the penal institution, the inmate receives clothes and toilet articles; he is assigned a cell and equipped with the necessary bedding, cutlery, and so forth. He is told what he can and cannot do, what is correct, and what is forbidden. He is expected to obey the rules and heed the orders of the superiors. If he is ill, he will be treated; he will be fed and assigned work. He is freed from all thought and cares, which are now the domain of the institution.

The prisoner suffers in particular from the fact that he "is being treated." Self-inflicted injuries, sickness, refusal to work, or hunger strikes oblige the administration to embark upon particular measures as regards the prisoner. The fact that the administration reacts to this type of behavior for all practical purposes strengthens it.

The inmates reveal a special tendency to describe their treatment by the administration by using the passive voice: I was pulled out, I was taken, I was beaten, I was punished, etc.[37] Stories presented in this form are often the essence of conversations held among the inmates. The necessity for the administration to react to the misconduct of the prisoners nourishes a specifically understood form of courage, and it assists and sustains a lack of responsibility for oneself. At the same time, because of its obligation, the administration is punished since the inmates force it to take care of them and create a type of work for which the administration is held responsible. The greater the number of such cases, the worse the institution's evaluation. Hence the administration treats acts of aggression and self-aggression on the part of the inmates as afflictions and would like to avoid them. This is a second reason why the prisoners seek refuge in both forms of aggression in order to win something for themselves.[38]

Exploitation and Violence, or Imposed Symbiosis

The attitude of the functionaries toward
the inmates of institution B

Generally speaking the opinion expressed by the staff is dominated by: (1) doubting the possibility of resocializing recidivists who should be retained in penal institutions; (2) the conviction that there is harsh social condemnation of the recidivist and demands by society for the repression of multiple offenders; society, in the eyes of the functionaries, expects this and leaves the convicts "at the mercy" of the prison staff.[39]

These conceptions justify in practice the forms and ways of realizing the two basic didactic functions which should be fulfilled by the prison in relation to the convicts, that is, discipline and turning work into a habit. Discipline turns into repression against the inmates ("trampling"), and work turns into ordinary "exploitation."

Actually, all the prisoners are "trampled" and in a certain way "exploited." But their reaction to this sort of attitude on the part of the prison staff varies. Those prisoners who do not allow themselves to be "exploited" are "trampled" to an even greater degree and vice versa. The reaction of the prisoners to this sort of treatment makes it possible to distinguish four categories of inmates: the "trampled," the opportunists ("sitting quietly"), the informers, and the "exploited" (providing services and producers).

THE CONVICTION ABOUT THE SOCIAL CONDEMNATION OF THE RECIDIVISTS

In the eyes of the staff, recidivists are "social outcasts." Society does not accept their presence among the "free people" and demands repressions. During one of the inmates' protests (in this particular penal institution) which constituted a refusal to work (a strike in the prison workshop), the prisoners called for improved work conditions (clothes, the reduction of production quotas, higher food allowances). The representative of the authorities of the penal institution tried to persuade the inmates to stop the protest by referring to public opinion, which (in his opinion) "calls for a biological destruction of recidivists." He described the conditions in which the inmates are housed and work as good compared to the conditions which society demands for offenders. Complaints from the inmates about various hardships—for example, the thickness of the tin (at variance with technological norms) or the physically exhausting nature of the work—are often rejected or summed up, as in the case mentioned: "You are here to make things difficult for us." The staff members regard themselves as the executors of social will and believe that "even a lame cur wouldn't care about the prisoners."

DOUBTING THE POSSIBILITY OF THE RESOCIALIZATION OF RECIDIVISTS

Functionaries of a lower level (guards and other workers of the security department) claim that "one has to harass and starve the crooks because they are degenerates of the highest caliber." "They are useless in society. Crooks are good-for-nothing free-loaders, and as soon as they leave prison, they return here" (head guard). "The best socialization of all took place in 1973 . . . when six of them completely resocialized. They left via the back entrance, feet first" (an officer of the security department describing a year when six of the convicts committed suicide). "Recidivists cannot be socialized. They should be kept in prison and destroyed. Those who can be exploited should be forced to work and the rest should be trampled" (a counselor). "Now I work at the gate, but when I was with them I used to talk out of curiosity. There were some with life sentences, but they never seemed to mind. I can't believe that they could be educated" (a guard).

The staff in this particular penal institution are not supporters of amnesty. They believe "sooner or later they (the inmates) will return here. This depends on how quickly they get caught." They give numerous examples of inmates who "returned" to the penal institution twice or three times ("old acquaintances"). Neither do they favor conditional release. "The longer he sits the less evil he will do outside." A motion for conditional release or the support for it are not the result of reflections on chances for re-offense but depend on the "merits" demonstrated in the penal institution.

"EXPLOITATION"

"Those who can be exploited should be made to work, and the rest—trampled." The administration tries to exploit all the convicts in various ways:

1. Using the services of the inmates: the functionaries have the prisoners perform even the most menial chores ("Wash a glass," "Hand me the

book," "Sharpen a pencil," "Slave! The chair"—"Here you are, O Master," etc.).

2. Stealing: often the functionaries conduct body searches and search the cells. Money and items which they regard as useful are simply appropriated. The staff members also search packages sent to the convicts and take prohibited articles. The inmates claim that the functionaries steal the contents. They also appropriate contraband.

3. The extortion of money and goods: some of the staff members write "false reports" (motions for punishing a prisoner for behavior contrary to the regulations). Before such a report is handed over to the warden, it lies on the desk of the one making the report, e.g., the head guard. The guard tells the inmate, "I've written you up." "For what?" "Not 'for what,' but 'why.' " This means (it could be in these words or another form) that the report could remain unsubmitted if the inmate were to give the guard some "faience" (for example, a hunting knife) or money. The prisoner must therefore either produce the mentioned knife or obtain the money (for example, through illegal correspondence). The money then can be thrown on the floor discreetly next to the passing guard (the author of the report): "Sir, you've dropped your money" (he scoops it off the floor and hands it over). "Hm, only a hundred złoty?" "Let's see, maybe more fell down" (he looks at the floor, pretending that he is searching, bends down and hands the guard another hundred złoty). "There was still another hundred złoty." "Alright, now fuck off."

The "hunt" could be even more profitable: the guard quietly steals toward the door to one of the cells and quickly opens it (the inmates are caught unawares): "Aha, no one got up" (when a functionary enters a cell all the inmates are obliged to get up, stand at attention and then the elder of the cell makes a report). "You're all going to be written up." For the prisoners it is quite clear why they will be written up and how they could "liquidate it."

Those inmates who refuse to produce or deliver the article can expect vengeance. They are often searched, which makes all trade impossible, their requests are rejected, etc. "He told me to bring some plates from the warehouse. I did this but he wrote me up anyway and I got a single (solitary confinement). He's getting revenge because I didn't get him a spring and some axes before."

4. Encouraging theft: the "screws" working in the wards (i.e., the pavilions occupied by the prisoners) do not accompany the inmates to the workshops and often propose that the inmates steal (work clothes, tools,

raw material, etc.) in return for some commodities, or they blackmail the inmates with a report.

5. "Squealing": many of the inmates are in different ways forced or encouraged to inform the staff about the situation in the institution. There is also a group of informers who provide these services of their own free will.

The inmates who agree to be exploited are classified as "squealers" (informers); or the "exploited" (inmates who perform service for the penal institution and the functionaries as well as illegal producers of "faience").

"INFORMING"

The convicts who are of some use to the prison staff are treated the best. There are therefore always some inmates who begin to inform and expect to be treated better than the other convicts. They also count on not being punished or at least punished more leniently for misconduct, and on receiving additional discharge.

Not only those inmates who are willing to inform the prison staff become informers. According to some of the functionaries, "it is a bad thing if the convict is well-adjusted because if he is maladjusted he can be forced to squeal." The inmate could become an informer if he is caught at some misdemeanor, as for instance: producing "faience"—if the article is valuable or made out of expensive and unobtainable raw material and its production is severely penalized; delivering a large amount of tea; other serious disciplinary misdeeds.

The avoidance of harsh penalties can be sufficient motive to accept a proposal to "squeal," or the fact that punishment could deprive the prisoner of chances for conditional release in the near future.

The "squealers" can be divided into informers who work for the security department and those who work for the penitentiary department. The former include those who inform the guards (the noncommissioned officers) and those who work for the directors of the department (the officers— the warden and his deputy, the commanders of pavilions). A similar division can be made among the informers of the penitentiary department—the informers of the directors of the department and of the counselors.

"Informers" of the lower level, the so-called squealers of the guards and the counselors usually provide information about the convicts (who drinks "tea," where the tea came from, who has "faience," who the leaders of the "people" are and what they do, who drinks vodka and where they get it).

The informers of the directors of the security department and the penitentiary department are expected to supply information about the prison staff as well as the "civil" workers (teachers, employees of the prison workshops) and their contacts with the convicts (who drinks vodka during working hours, who trades and with whom, what is being bartered, the close rapport between the convicts and the functionaries). Of course, the most important information for the administration of the penal institution concerns moods among the convicts and the functionaries, planned escapes or protests.

An interesting, albeit very small, category are informers of the penitentiary department "slipped" into the security department to purposefully misinform about the work of the penitentiary department, and vice versa. This category reflects the conflicts between the two departments.

The staff members do not write reports if they know that the convict concerned is an informer. If however, unaware of his function, they do so, then the report never reaches the warden because, for example, the head of the security "hides it on the way." Reports about informers written by the workers in production enterprises "get lost somewhere in the ward."

As I have already mentioned, the "squealers" expect to be conditionally released in return for the delivered information. Often the functionaries promise the convicts as early as during their enlistment that a motion for conditional discharge will be forwarded to court. The lower-level functionaries who make this sort of a promise actually have very limited opportunities for inducing the authorities of the penal institution to support or present a motion for conditional release. This is why they frequently lie to the inmates by telling them that their plea will be presented in the near future. Shortly before a forthcoming court sitting they "pack the informer off and send him to another prison."

"Exploited" prisoners can be divided into four categories:

1. The cooks, barbers, librarians, corridor orderlies, employees of the radio network (unpaid) who perform additional work apart from that which they are formally obliged to do. The functionaries also commission them to make tea, keep the official accounts, clean uniforms, cut hair, etc.

2. Secondary school graduates, inmates with a profession, or those who are able to repair various equipment. Depending on their skills, they perform different jobs for the functionaries (repairing vacuum cleaners and

irons, doing auto-body repairs, spray painting cars, doing school assignments for prison-staff students of the penitentiary school, and working as foremen in production).

3. Inmates who possess manual skills and are able to produce various ornaments or useful articles, for example powder compacts or miniature pianos.

4. Convicts who work in the metal shops and make such articles as hunting knives, switchblade knives, axes, cleavers, or flower stands illegally, using the available machines. This group delivers the finished articles ("faience") to some of the functionaries in return for payment. They, in turn, resell them profitably to residents of the nearby town or to acquaintances.

Those inmates who allow themselves to be exploited are treated much more leniently than the "trampled" and "those who sit quietly." Their offenses are ignored and "if someone squeals or moonlights, we can settle the matter under certain conditions."

The better the informers and "exploited" of the high-ranking personnel play their roles, the greater their significance in the prison community. Some of these inmates are actually more important than the lower-level staff members. The latter fear these prisoners but are unable to act to their detriment, aware of the fact that the inmates remain under the protection of the superiors and are untouchable. These two categories of members of the prison community dislike each other and fight against each other.

Prisoner W was a school janitor. He was also an informer for the deputy director of the security department who was much feared by all prisoners and guards. W was also a "peddler" who bought up "faience" and sold tea to the inmates (purchased at retail prices and sold at prices specific for the prison). Since he had a greater opportunity of movement in the institution than the other inmates, he distributed various objects for payment and carried messages or money. W was also a very conscientious janitor who by working well and performing many helpful jobs (painting walls, making small repairs) remained useful for the administration. He also informed—and had his own network of informers, who were frequently unaware of their function. At the same time, W "made deals" and bartered. For this reason the guards wanted to "cut him down." But W remained clever and did not allow them to catch him committing a misdemeanor. The guards harassed him and made him work harder, and they criticized what he had already done. For example, one guard publicly charged W with "peddling, lounging around, and wandering wherever he wants to," insulted him, and threatened that "all this must cease." W informed the warden, reminding him that he worked well and could not tolerate public accusations. When the warden asked whether the charges of peddling were true, his reply was: "No one has caught me, so what's the problem?" The director of the security department summoned the guard, expressed his anger, and threatened that in the future the guard would be transferred for such behavior. From that time the guard "was meek" and reproached the prisoner for informing on him quite unnecessarily since he (the guard) "was only joking" and actually "has nothing against him and everything is in order."

W was more useful for the deputy director of the security department than the guard and was protected by the director's authority. Enjoying such protection, he was able to develop his trade which was basically quite safe for the administration and provided W with the opportunity to penetrate prison life and gather information.

"TRAMPLING"

All the prisoners are to a certain degree "trampled," but this concerns most of all those who are of no official or private use to the staff. This "trampling" by the prison staff is experienced by all the inmates.

Offending the prisoners ("you're a thief"). The prison staff often do not address the inmates in ways other than "you thief, you bandit, you thug, you whore, you fucked cock," etc.

Malice and bullying ("I have to endure this patiently"). Inmates who are placed in solitary confinement for refusing to work are additionally punished (in accordance with the rules valid at the time of my investigations) by decreasing their food allowances. This penalty consisted of denying the inmates soup one day and the second course on the following day, until the end of the assigned term. Each meal served was noted down so that those on duty the next day would know what the inmate had received. Sometimes a guard would tell the guard on duty to serve the second course despite the fact that this had been given on the previous day. When the prisoner was given his meal, happy because the second course is always better, the guard would kick the bowl, spilling its contents on the inmate. He then would laugh and jeer and order the inmate not to cheat and to remember what is his due.

The inmates were also served spoiled sausage for supper and would suffer from diarrhea. The cells have only a single bucket for excrement. If one of the prisoners was using it, then the rest relieved themselves in the "corners." The guards laughed, calling the inmates "cattle, with no culture," who "shit wherever possible, or more convenient," "brought up in a pig sty," etc.

Often a functionary gets upset. The inmates are sensitive to the current mood of the personnel and know that if they "come across" a nervous staff member something unpleasant might happen. They pass on the information that functionary Y is "mad" and "looking for a fight in order to let off steam." No one that day will settle any of his affairs (request, motions, etc.) with Y.

The functionaries are well aware of their "weaknesses," and in a perverse way exploit each other in order to aggravate the prisoners or make fun of their own colleagues. They might, for example, inform inmate Y that he is summoned by functionary X (although nothing of the sort took place). Y reports to X, X grows furious, insults Y and throws him out of the room. Those who played this joke observe the whole incident from afar and laugh at their colleague. If they do not follow the course of the event directly, then they have a topic for conversations about X and imagine how "he got mad," "cursed Y" and even "slugged him."

Body searches and searches of the cells also aggravate the inmates. The staff use this opportunity to take away items which the inmates are permitted or not forbidden to have and to which the inmates are emotionally attached (family photographs, drawings, poems). Such malevolent deprivation is particularly painful for the prisoners.

Group responsibility ("I am always guilty"). Often the identity of the guilty party is not even established, but all the inmates who could have committed the offense (breaking a chair, a table, a radio, etc.) are punished. If two of the prisoners are fighting, both are punished in the same way, without finding out who began the fight, who was merely defending himself, and who attacked first.

Breaking the will of the prisoners ("it is the way I say it is," "I am never right," "I do what they tell me to"). If the convict argues with a functionary that some job assignment is senseless, the functionary will order him to do it anyway ("Wash the floor." "It was washed." "Then wash it again." "These shoes are dirty." "But they're clean." "Dirty." "Yes, they're dirty." "This coffee is unsweetened." "But it was sweetened with sugar." "Yes, it's sweet").

Inmate M wanted to leave his cell and go to the recreation hall at a time when he was usually permitted to watch television; he asked the guard through the door: "Please, sir, could I go now?" "Call me Caesar, and I'll let you go." "Caesar, sir, let me out." This and other conversations were the reason why the guard began to be called "Caesar" by the inmates.

Beating ("I never know when I'll get it on the head"). Inmates admitted from another prison to institution B are "welcomed" by the functionaries. Whether they are beaten depends on the reason for their transfer. If, for instance, it was connected with participation in a riot or with bad conduct, then they are usually beaten (the "welcome"). Another criterion can be participation in "hidden life"—for example, "git people" are beaten. Still another reason is the article of the penal code under which the prisoner was accused—for example, aggressive crimes (robbery, etc.).

Unyielding in the face of manipulation ("I will never win"). A prisoner who is harassed by other inmates can legally ask for another cell. If he is refused by the administration and continues to be harassed, he has only self-inflicted injuries or a hunger strike at his disposal to achieve his goal. The administration of the penal institution reacts severely to such behavior. Not only does it uphold its earlier decisions but also penalizes the inmate. In the future it can persecute him in revenge for his attempt at "blackmail."

As mentioned earlier, some of the inmates are "trampled" much more than others. They include those who are particularly hostile toward the prison staff and toward the prisoners, those who are subservient to the functionaries, and those who do not cooperate with the administration.

In the eyes of the prison staff, this category of prisoners is characterized by their refusal to cooperate in any way with the administration. They reveal predispositions for playing the role of leaders, participators in "hidden life," they refuse to work, file official complaints against the functionaries, and are aggressive toward the staff. As a rule these convicts have more punishments "on their record" than the rest. The functionaries aggravate and watch them more than the others and provoke misconduct for which they are penalized. All their requests or pleas are rejected. The particularly dangerous, hard, stubborn, and fearless inmates who do not hide their animosity toward the administration are "trampled" by the functionaries permanently: they are the "trampled" in the true sense of the word.

The inmates who are hostile toward the administration but who, in contrast to the "trampled," do not reveal their feelings or avoid direct conflicts with the functionaries, do not fall into disgrace as often as the "trampled." The functionaries keep an eye on them, but these inmates "sit quietly"—they are known as "opportunists."

The "trampled" openly express their hostility to the administration. They despise the subservience of certain inmates toward the staff, and they condemn informers and those who cooperate with the functionaries. They have "character" and are unyielding. They also try to maintain the principles of divisions among the prisoners which stem from the norms of "hidden life." The functionaries have special methods of combating this group of inmates. They mainly strive to constantly punish them ("the moment I leave solitary confinement, I go back") by means of various forms of confinement: "the hard bed," solitary confinement, or the "straps." The inmates who are already isolated are "finished off mentally and physically." These methods could lead to suicide or break down the resistance of the prisoner. The particular stages of this process are:

1. Premises for punishment—as narrated by the "trampled" prisoners. "They use any possible pretext to write reports and severely punish." "For a missing button a screw will hit you in the face or write a report." "Those who stand up for themselves are provoked, the screw will curse and they will throw themselves on him with fists." For this misconduct the inmate can be beaten, in addition to being sent to solitary confinement or being put in "straps." "Everything is correct from the formal point of view—the punishment is justified—but they are the reason why a man behaves in such a way."

2. The administration of punishment—as narrated by the "trampled." *Straps.* To be tied up with a triple safety strap is not disciplinary punishment but a measure for making the inmate immobile when he has "gone crazy" as evidenced by the fact that he "threw himself at the functionaries with his fists."

"Using the strap" involves placing the prisoner on a wooden bed, with his arms outstretched. His limbs and head are fastened to the edge of the bed in such a way that by pulling the straps to which they are attached, the inmate is stretched "to the four corners of the world." Then, the straps are placed across the chest and hips and when pulled tight, they press the trunk to the boards of the bed. The convict is thus rendered completely immobile. The pressure of the straps causes pain, and some of the inmates unwillingly defecate and urinate. Sometimes they faint, losing and regaining consciousness. Eventually, they grow numb.

The application of the straps is accompanied by various "improvisations." The inmate (often battered because he resisted having the straps tied) is put on a bed drenched with water or wrapped in a wet sheet so that he suffers from blisters. He has a headrest under his back, and a bowl of hot soup is often placed on his chest (so that "he can eat a bit"), which burns him until the soup grows cool. In the summer the window is open so that flies crawl on his immobile body. After being untied, the inmate experiences intermittent periods of paralysis of the limbs.

Solitary confinement cell. Because of a conflict with a guard, J. W. was punished with three months of solitary confinement. He was promised that "he would never leave alive." Every evening he placed a stool under the door of the cell. On it he put a wash bowl which leaned against the door, and he spent the nights in "terror, waiting for their visit." He heard the guards entering cells close to his own in the solitary confinement ward and overheard the cries and groans of the beaten inmates, but he was spared.

A "night visit" of the guards consists of silently entering the cell of the convict, surprising him while he is asleep and assaulting him. Sometimes, such punishment results in a loss of consciousness; then water is poured over the bed and the window left open, especially in winter. The prisoner, weak from the beating, soon becomes ill (pneumonia, influenza).

Beating. "They beat until the blood flows and then tell us to wash the floor." "The screws beat us and then ask us to kiss their hands." "They drag or throw us down the stairs." If the inmate is seriously "beaten by the screws, they send him to solitary confinement and let him out when he gets better"—and attempts to obtain an official medical examination are futile. As a rule, the guards try to assault the inmates in such a way as not to leave traces on their bodies. This makes it impossible to perform a medical examination. Popular methods of assault include:

- "Bombardment"—beating the entire body with fists: "I was returning from a walk. I was on IV. They called me to come to III. There were four of them. At the beginning I didn't know what was happening but suspected something. They found a stick in the lavatory and led me to the sickbay. 'Lie down on the stool.' 'I won't. I'm not even guilty.' They wanted to force me but I didn't allow them so they bombarded me and I got it in the kidneys, too. I rushed out into the corridor, you were there and they gave up."
- "Barrels"—to beat with fists along the kidneys.
- "Board laying"—four functionaries hold the inmate by his limbs, place his underbelly on a stool and the fifth functionary beats his buttocks with a board.
- "Crumbling"—a truncheon is used to hit the ligaments of the anus, and the inmate defecates.

If by chance there are any traces of the assault and the inmate wishes to request an official medical examination, the functionaries bribe or blackmail him. The examination itself is performed by a female assistant surgeon and is rather useless since she is the wife of the head of the security department and is unwilling to incriminate her husband, who is responsible for the work of his guards.

3. A break down. Inmate W. H. claims that sometimes during his stay in solitary confinement, he did not receive his meals. He was beaten and told that he "would never get out alive." After some time he became depressed and contemplated suicide, thinking that he "could not stand it any longer." One day the door to his cell opened, in came a "screw and threw me a noose, saying 'You're supposed to hang tomorrow.' " "Sometimes one can't take it any longer and hangs oneself."

As a result of the treatment described above, many of the inmates changed their attitudes and became "opportunists," "those who sit quietly." Others began to "cooperate with the screw," but such a sudden improvement of relations with the functionaries is quickly noticed by the other inmates and appropriately interpreted. Still others break down and commit suicide. Only a few during their entire stay in prison maintain their convictions and remain "full of character" until the end.

"THOSE WHO SIT QUIETLY" (OPPORTUNISTS)

These inmates are decidedly hostile to the prison staff but never show it. Just like the "trampled," they are contemptuous of cooperation with the staff and of those convicts who agree to such cooperation. Many of them take part in "hidden life." They believe that "there is no sense in taking a risk. Why should one lose one's health and nerves?" and they carry out the orders issued by the functionaries so as to avoid conflicts. They also avoid committing any serious offenses against the rules, aware that the administration "has its eye on them." Conduct contrary to the regulations is usually kept very secret.

The prison staff considers "those who sit quietly" as rather well behaved. They are punished less frequently, but this does not mean that they are rewarded more often than others. This group of inmates, moreover, does not allow itself to be provoked by the staff.

The attitudes of the prisoners toward functionaries in institution B

The inmates regard the functionaries as lazy and unintelligent. The personnel is supposedly recruited from people who, in the prisoners' opinion, were unsuitable for work in other institutions, either because they were underqualified, both professionally and mentally, or because of "inborn" laziness. The inmates claim that the functionaries often had been fired from their previous places of employment and came to the penal institution because it offered good wages.

"These are mainly small-scale farmers; they have land and come here to make additional money—and they make quite a lot." "That one was a militiaman. They threw him out and he found himself here." "X was a janitor." "Y could not find a decent job." "Some of them here are illiterates . . . that one does not know how to read. One day the boys were talking in the cell and he shouted: 'Cell 68, quiet!' They began to laugh and he repeated: 'Quiet in cell 68.' They laughed even more and he wrote them up. The next day the officer on duty asked what happened: everyone became speechless, including the head guard, because this was the wrong cell. He had mixed up 68 with 86. Later on it turned out that he can't count. But the boys got written up anyway."

"This one can't read or write. When he wants to write a report he calls me and says: 'I'll dictate because I forgot my glasses.' "

"One day it was the same with the letters. Whenever he is supposed to hand out the mail, he tells me to read who it's for. Once he took a letter and read out some name, Kowalski or something like that, and there's no one here with that name. I looked at it and said: 'That's for me.' "

". . . Officers? No education needed here, just good will. . . . Now they're finishing some sort of a secondary school. Some of the prisoners do their homework for them. The head people supposedly have some higher education. When one of them does, then you can see it right away in the cultured way he speaks. But if he's a son of a bitch then nothing helps . . . that deputy of the warden, he has no college education, he's a former secret police agent, and when the secret police was dissolved, he moved to the penal system."

"What kind of people are they, anyway, their wives leave them and run away with others. . . ." "You can see right away what that one could have been looking for in life. He's a born cheat." "They envy us for what we had outside."

"Since they were useless for any other sort of work, then they can live it up and show off here." "These aren't people, they're bandits." "Reptiles." "So what if I'm working here. . . . I can work . . . but what are those sons of bitches doing here? Why is he allowed to do anything he likes? Why do regulations apply only to me? Put them up against the wall and shoot them all." "I can't do it here, but the minute I'm out, I'll settle accounts with some of them." "Big shots . . . they beat us and then want us to thank them. "This is what justice of the Red Spiders is all about." "One of them told us to call him Napoleon." "They stand like that all day and talk, doing nothing." "If one of them gets bored or scared because he is doing nothing at all, then he'll summon some inmate who happens to be handy and yell at him that he has grown lazy and doesn't button up. Then peace reigns again, he's shown that he's watchful, in other words, that he works and doesn't loaf around. Their work is just to make a lot of noise." "The decent ones leave you alone and some even don't like what the others are doing. But so what? Will he deal with them? They would settle him for good, and why should he bother?"

"TO TRICK"

One must act in such a way as to avoid punishment and responsibility, and to reap some benefits. The methods depend on the situation:

1. "Pushing bull," "pumping," "fibbing": fabricating stories about oneself, boasting. Prisoners do this in order to place themselves in a favorable light, to endear themselves to the guards, evoking respect or fear. This method also includes falsifying events, often in order to conceal something or to avoid punishment.

2. Creating a diversion, for instance, a meeting or interesting conversation, in order to avert the attention of the guards; a method applied to pass an illegal message, throw out a prohibited item during a search, etc.

3. Simulating cooperation: giving the impression that one knows much about the "relationships among the inmates" and is willing to inform the guard if he agrees to concessions. In reality, the information concerns misdemeanors committed by inmates who are not liked, who interfere in deals, or who harass others. Sometimes fabricated information is given because they do not know the relationships.

4. Playing the role of the well-behaved inmate who resocializes himself "in order to arouse the interest of the counselor who will then strive for further success in resocialization." This is often connected with lenient treatment of the inmate, commissioning unpaid work (e.g., the bulletin board) which involves a partial departure from the daily routine.

5. Disarmament involves being pleasant to the functionaries, complimenting them, displaying submissive behavior, telling jokes on favorite topics, for instance, sex: "Do you remember when Boguska was here [a "fag"]? Well, she used to deal with three men at once . . . she would bend over, one would fuck her in the mouth, the other in the ass, and she

would jack-off the third one.'' The prisoner told this story in a colorful way, demonstrating the positions to the guard who listened attentively, laughed, and did not restrain the storyteller or the other inmates.

The inmates gladly allow the functionaries to escort them to the cells of the ''fags'' to engage in sexual intercourse, i.e., so that the functionary can watch through the peephole.

The purpose of disarming the staff is usually to change the mood or create an atmosphere of lightheartedness and absence of hostility in which the functionaries find it difficult to be demanding and rigorous.

6. Corruption can include promising the staff ''faience,'' offering ''gifts,'' reselling tea, for example, paying to send uncensored letters.

7. Dependence is accomplished mainly by those prisoners who do unpaid work. Besides doing their own jobs as well as possible, they do jobs for the staff—making tea, keeping records, passing chairs, cleaning a room, ''informing,'' cutting hair, doing laundry, ironing uniforms, sewing, etc. The staff grow accustomed to using the prisoners and become lazy, unable to manage without their helpers. This causes the staff to make various concessions and decisions favorable to the inmates.

8. One should not distinguish oneself. ''Once you expose yourself, they'll remember you.'' ''It is better to behave like the majority of the convicts—then they don't have any reason to pay special attention to you.'' ''Just follow the others.''

An inmate who has received rewards which are recognized as a sign of cooperation with the administration will be condemned by the other inmates. This discourages many of the prisoners from competing for the reward. But they also avoid being punished. Many of the inmates try to be seen as rarely as possible by the functionaries, to keep out of their sight, ''to hide.'' If such a convict notices that he is being observed by a staff member, he moves to another spot. He also prefers to stand in the second row during roll call, to march in the center of the column, and to keep silent in the presence of a functionary. Asked by the latter about other inmates or certain events, his reply suggests that he saw and knows nothing. He carries out his assigned jobs diligently, giving no pretext for drawing attention to himself. He also rarely complains or has any requests.

''TO STAND UP FOR YOURSELF''

1. ''You have to stand up for yourself and not let yourself be mucked, trampled, or sold—you have to defend your honor.'' ''If he swears at you,

then give it back to him." "A screw calls me 'peasant,' and I say: 'You're the peasant, taken away from the plow.' " "But you can't let yourself be provoked, because if he curses you on purpose and you hit him, then he will immediately send for the boys from the gate and you will get the straps."

2. "When he pulls a false report on you, then you should appeal to the warden, but some are afraid to do that because they could get written up for unfounded complaints."

3. The prisoners put curses on the functionaries. On Christmas Eve they say: "May you share a roof tile (instead of the traditional wafer)," and on other occasions: "May you not live to see another day."

4. Minimum effort—maximum discontentment: "No one carries out orders because they want to, only to get the screw off his back." The majority of the inmates try to meet the production norms and no more. Sometimes they do not even make that effort and endeavor to find a suitable excuse. According to the inmates the "norms" are intentionally higher in order to exploit the prisoners as much as possible. The functionaries distrust the inmates and believe that they will not fulfill the norms intentionally (out of both laziness and hostility toward the functionaries); thus with the raised norms the functionaries hope to achieve the "normal ones." Other orders are carried out slowly and to a minimal degree but enough so that a trace of the work always remains which would be proof to contradict any eventual claims that nothing had been done.

Any sort of work is accompanied by discontentment: "Too much work," "Why me?" "This is impossible and cannot be done," etc. By minimizing the effort, one maximizes the discontentment.

5. The prisoners often tell the staff what they think about "what they are doing to us" and enumerate their grievances. The staff takes offense to these lists of grievances and injustices and maintains that the prisoners lie or exaggerate. The prisoners threaten to take them to court after their release.

6. Self-inflicted injuries: a prisoner who believes that a "report" calling for punishment for misconduct is unfair can inflict injuries on himself. This special resoluteness serves to manifest the wrong he has suffered. The inmate also protests against what, in his opinion, are unfounded accusations and protects himself against injustice.

The administration is reluctant to grant requests for transfer to another cell by an inmate who has been harassed in the cell by the other inmates.

The administration claims that an agreement to this type of a plea could result in a "migration" of the inmates involving all the cells in the institution. This is why the desperate inmate who has been denied his request seeks refuge in self-mutilation in order to force the administration to make concessions.

An inmate who deals a blow and insults a staff member in the presence of other functionaries and inmates is severely punished, for example, by solitary confinement. Once there, he can expect a "visit" from the guards who take revenge for the dishonor. In fear of the impending beating, he cuts his veins and smears himself with blood to avoid retaliation. Self-mutilation, therefore, can be used to manipulate the staff's behavior toward the prisoner.

The reaction of the personnel to the attitude of the prisoners described above is, for the inmates, the basis for distinguishing several categories of functionaries. Generally the division includes those who "*let you live,*" and those who "*make life difficult*" ("we are here to make your life difficult").

Those who "let you live" are the functionaries who cause "no harm." The latter "closes his eyes to the prisoners' various nonregulation affairs," "doesn't show off how great he is," "doesn't swell up," "even if he writes a report then for a good reason," ". . . doesn't help but doesn't interfere either."

But there are also functionaries who *help,* who "talk like a human being," "offer advice," "support a request," "sometimes close their eyes to something slightly off," "propose conditional release if one deserves it." The "helpers" often include but are not limited to the counselors.

Those who "let you live" also include those who "go for more." With them one can do deals. They provide large amounts of tea and cigarettes and receive money from the outside. Of course, they also earn something this way, but they take risks and are "sometimes denounced."

The inmates and the staff of the penal institution involved in these sorts of transactions have a close relationship. This is also how various information is channeled, for example, who among the prisoners "squeals," or for which inmate is the administration "preparing something" and what does that "something" involve.

The term *reptiles* refers to those who "make life difficult" in a particularly obvious way. The "reptiles" (but not only they) like to demonstrate their "omnipotence." Even though they could go around a column of marching inmates, they go straight through it; they force groups of prisoners to stand aside. "They don't see us because we are nothing to them." They also often "look for a fight," and it is said that such a staff member "is sick if he doesn't slug somebody during his shift." This group includes members of the staff whom the inmates call "Policeman," "Gooseneck," "SS-man," "Auschwitz man," "Kapo."

The "reptiles" demonstrate the greatest initiative in writing reports, often "for even the slightest thing." It is they who most often carry out beatings and, according to the prisoners, enjoy doing so. Sometimes the prisoner is faced with the alternative: "what would you prefer, a write-up or five slugs?" As a rule the inmates choose the beating because "it doesn't leave traces and the paper remains" in the files. "Reptiles" are universally known and most feared by the inmates. They become prison legends, are recalled after transfer to another prison, and are compared with other infamous "reptiles."

The inmates consider staff members who "do nothing themselves and one has to work for them" as those who "make life difficult." The "good-for-nothings" fail to perform their duties properly. They shorten exercise periods or forbid the inmates to go outside "because they don't feel like standing in the courtyard to watch us." They also demand that everything be done for them—a chair given or a cigarette handed, another inmate summoned. "They laze around for hours," but sometimes this is to the inmates' advantage. During visiting hours, for example, the good-for-nothings prefer to talk with the other functionaries rather than watch the inmates. They also make fewer searches.

Not all of them, however, are so passive. Many, without cooperating with the inmates, "live off them." "They subsist on extorting faience," "on searches or false reports" ("I'll write you up unless you make a deal with me"). They also appropriate various items or money found during cell searches and act like vultures.

The "vultures" do not trade with the inmates because they are afraid of being denounced. They are very careful: inmate X made a set of hunting knives and an axe, which were taken away during a search, with a report that he had been smuggling parts of the knives. These parts, however, were appropriated much earlier. The inmate in an interview with the warden claimed that something quite different was taken, but this only led to additional punishment for slandering a staff member.

Mutual Profits from Co-existence

Serving a sentence in the conditions of a semi-open institution (work center) is associated with special tasks for the administration of those units. One of the primary tasks is to employ the prisoners for a certain number of working hours. The administration must make an agreement with enterprises located nearby so that, when faced with a labor shortage, they will employ the inmates. In the region in which institution C is situated, the need for workers is considerable, and demand for the inmates' labor is greater than can be met by the local penal institutions. This creates a favorable situation for the administration. It is obliged only to employ for a certain number of working hours, according to an annual plan, and therefore can select the enterprises to which it wishes to send the inmates.[40] The fulfillment of the plan by the given enterprise often depends on the number of employees, which puts it in a situation of being the one to take the initiative to employ the inmates. The prison administration, therefore, has no problem finding employment for the inmates and thus fulfilling its plans.

Since the inmates work outside the prison, strict control by the prison staff is impossible. The workers are scattered in various state enterprises. Nonetheless, their conduct is scrutinized by the functionaries. Control in these conditions is accomplished through the so-called patrol system when the functionaries visit the places of employment. For example, inmates engaged in building roads remain under the surveillance of a suitable number of guards depending on the size of the group. Of course, just as in the penal institutions, prisoner-informers are also used for the purposes of control.

Inmates employed outside the prison face many temptations: escape, access to alcohol, theft, barter, etc. But in their places of work they remain in full sight of the civil workers and the management, who judge their behavior and work.

The administration of the penal institution has responsibility for the discipline of the work parties. For this reason it is very sensitive about opinions concerning the inmates, and its attitude toward them depends on that opinion to a large degree. A lack of complaints or displeasure on the part of the enterprise which employs the prisoners is the minimum demanded by the guards. An eventual positive opinion is regarded, above all, as the result of the good work performed by the prison staff. The inmates, therefore, are supposed to act in such a way as not to undermine the good opinion of institution C, and the broad margin of freedom enjoyed by them is to be used in such a way as not to make any problems for the administration. Otherwise, this freedom would be withdrawn and the disobedient inmates employed in the penal institution, with all its negative consequences.

What determines the attitude of the functionaries toward a prisoner is thus not so much his membership in an informal group of the "code users" as his participation in formulating the opinion about the work performed by the prisoner. Nonetheless, the "code users" are subject to even greater pressure than the other inmates. Good job assignments or at least support for conditional release depend on a resignation from the "code." This practice is also supported by penitentiary judges, upon whom the conditional discharge ultimately depends.[41] Those who resign from the "code" must stand in the corridor and loudly shout "fuck the code." The "curse" is an irreversible severance. After this, the penitentiary judge can be certain that the inmate will never return to the "code."

The inmates also watch each other so as not to lose profits offered by work outside the institution. The guards do not have to guard them much or sometimes not at all. An extreme example occurred when the inmates brought back to the prison a drunk guard, insensible, and armed with a machine gun. His task had been to escort the prisoners employed in building roads.

The consumption and abuse of alcohol also occurs among the prisoners, who sometimes wander off from the place of work. These incidents are most severely punished since they undermine the opinion among the local population regarding the work of the penitentiary administration.

Certain misdemeanors committed by the inmates are tolerated. The refusal to work, riots, escapes, hostility toward the functionaries, insubordination in places of work could result in their not being able to work in the local enterprises. This would signify the inability of the administration to accomplish its assigned tasks. Moreover, the administration itself would then lose the opportunity of exploiting the inmates. A semi-open institution makes it possible to use the inmates outside the prison as well as to exploit them for private purposes (the building of a camping trailer or a summer house, cleaning up the area around one's house, etc.), and not only those of the prison staff.[42] Just as sending the prisoner to work in a specific enterprise can be the object of informal deals and profitable for the administration (chiefly the management of the institution), so the hiring out of the prisoners to private persons can become an additional source of income. This is why relations between the guards and the prisoners are worked out in such a way as not to disrupt the profits of either side.

Variants of Relationships between the Prisoners and the Functionaries as an Outgrowth of the Relationships within the Prison Community

We have observed, not only in institution A, an evolution of the administration's attitude toward the informal organization of the prisoners: from a battle to eliminate it to the prevention of the most drastic symptoms of its functioning and the manipulation of relations governing it. This evolution developed together with the growing ineffectiveness of subsequent methods of combating "hidden life," whose selection were dictated by the fact that the causes of the emergence of "hidden life" were perceived as having developed outside the prison. The ineffectiveness of these methods finally led to the conviction that "hidden life" simply cannot be eliminated.

One is struck by a certain incohesion between the characteristic functions fulfilled by "hidden life" created by the prison system and the inclination of the prison system toward a transmission hypothesis of explaining "hidden life." It was indicated, in accordance with the spirit of this work, that "hidden life" is ". . . directed toward an optimalization of the various ways of satisfying the psychological and physiological needs of the detainees or the inmates serving their sentences, and in particular by forcing concessions from the staff and imposing exploitative pressure on the co-inmates. For example, the demands that the 'code users' demonstrate a ruthless attitude toward the 'suckers' and force them to give up clothes and bed linens, force them to clean up, to appropriate the goods they produced. . . ."[43] ". . . The code users establish the norms to be met and prohibit exceeding them; they force others to hand over the goods produced, etc."[44]

The prison system, however, has not made a clear statement about the causes of "hidden life." "Some of the authors perceive them to be rooted in the faulty educational system and staff shortages. . . . Others try to explain its causes by means of certain objective conditions which include aggression associated with confinement. Still others believe that this is a phenomenon imminently connected with the prison system as an institution. This is where it emerges and from here it is disseminated. The remaining authors are of the opinion that this phenomenon is not a product of the penitentiary but is transmitted into the prison from the outside by particular criminal groups."[45] Even if one comes across statements which indicate the source, they usually point to the area outside the prison system: "The essence of 'hidden life' and its specific mechanism distinctly indicate a transfer between that which is happening in the criminal groups, especially the juveniles, on the outside and that which we call the 'hidden life' in the penal institutions."[46]

Hypotheses of the transmission of "hidden life" into the penal institutions were persistently retained despite the notice taken of certain phenomena which negated them:

> I believe that elements of "hidden life" are transmitted into penal institutions from other areas of life, especially from the criminal environments. I notice, however, that certain norms of this subculture are modified. It is also difficult to agree with the statement that the phenomena of "hidden life" do not occur in the milieu of economic [white-collar] criminals. Nonetheless, long-term observation proves that the phenomenon in that category of prisoners is of a slightly different character.[47]

The recognition of "hidden life" as characteristic only for penal institutions for juvenile offenders is completely false and cannot be explained by the "mentality" of the juveniles. Let us once again recall a statement concerning this particular issue: "As far as I can remember, in the mid 1960s there were no such forms of 'hidden life' as there are now among recidivists and adults. . . . Formerly, twenty-one was some sort of a magical age beyond which the juvenile ceased to be connected with a criminal group and could become a normal convict. Now this has changed. . . ."[48]

The lack of an explanation for the causes, or support for the "transmission" hypothesis would provide an explanation of the concentration the prison system puts on overcoming the symptoms of "hidden life" since there is nothing else to be done. The assumption that "hidden life" is transmitted into the penal institution is an excuse not to seek the causes within the system of serving the prison sentence. It frees one from an eventual recognition of oneself as the guilty party responsible for the emergence of the whole phenomenon, as well as from formulating statements about the necessity of reforming the penal system or even abandoning this form of punishment which not only fails to accomplish its resocialization functions, but is inhumane as well. This would be like "cutting off the branch upon which one perches."

On the basis of my conception which explains the origin and functions of the informal organization of the inmates (emphasizing here a function which is similarly characterized by the prison system), I regard the ways in which the causes of "hidden life" are viewed by the penal system as incohesive with the functions indicated by it, and the placing of its sources "outside" the penal institutions (without negating certain arguments supporting this hypothesis) as instrumental, safeguarding the interests of the representatives of the penal system and serving as a rationalization which protects them against the perils indicated.

But this is only a partial answer to the query: why is the attitude of the prison staff defined only by the symptoms (results, functions) of "hidden life" without reference to its sources within the prison itself?

I. In those penal institutions where the main sources for obtaining goods by the prisoners (discussed in the previous chapter) are external, there is a strong polarization of the prison community. One group of convicts becomes the object of aggression and exploitation by the others. On the basis of this exploitation, a dichotomic structure of the prison community and the normative system which sanctions it appears. The laws which govern it are contrary to prison regulations and to the principles of confinement contained in the executive penal code. They are predominantly contrary to the premises about total control and subjection of the prisoners to the administration of a totalitarian institution. The reason for this is that "hidden life" creates a "second authority" in the prison which demands special rights for itself—the right to rule the community of the prisoners and the acceptance of this state of affairs by the administration. In reality, the acceptance of this second authority would signify the loss of a monopoly of power enjoyed by the prison staff. The latter cannot agree and embarks upon attempts to eliminate this self-established authority. This step, however, only leads toward the aggression of the inmates against the administration.

The object of the prisons' "tooling" is the person who has broken the law, who has refuted, by his behavior, the social order of which the prison is a representative and defender. To allow a second authority would be a direct contradiction to the principles of defense for which they were established. Penal institutions must be characterized by steadfast faith in their legitimacy.

The resistance of the prisoners to the prison order serves as evidence against the latter. This can be explained only by the evil immanent in the criminals themselves. A typical feature of representatives of the penal system is fatalism expressed in their conviction that resocializing the inmates is impossible, and in the popularity of a thesis about the biological determinants of criminal behavior; hence the popularity of the "transmission" theory of "hidden life." The recognition by the penal system that the prison gives rise to that which the system itself describes as the evil of "hidden life" would be a self-negation—how can a lawfully managed institution produce lawlessness? The weight of the facts proving this is possible is a source of shame for the prison and sometimes of the resultant aggression toward the inmates.

The explanation outlined above proposes a kind of psychoanalytical interpretation of the prison institution whose superego does not permit the disclosure of facts which undermine it. The prison creates its own subconsciousness.

In the course of my studies, it was precisely this resistance that the prison reality has against its recognition which brought to mind associations with psychoanalysis. I acted like a psychoanalyst who waits until the patient will talk about himself of his own free will—growing familiar with the prisoners and allowing myself to follow the associations which the prison wears. I recall this fact in connection with the attitudes of the functionaries toward "hidden life," since here there is also concern for controlling perception by persons from the outside.

To say that total control in prison is in opposition to the second authority to whose emergence it contributed in an involuntary way, would be only a half-truth. Total control is also concerned with not revealing this problem outside the prison, and, if that has already happened, then to influence the way it is perceived.[49]

I have stated that the administration of the penal institution also refused to agree to the existence of a second authority in the prison, but it is a fact that it does exist. The methods of breaking it up did not provide the expected results, and this led to a reconciliation with the existence of second authority, albeit subject to special control.

The evolution of attitudes toward "hidden life" can be illustrated rather well by referring to relations between, let us say, wolves, deer, and the forest ranger. The wolves live off the deer but this brutality of nature can be disturbing for the forest ranger. If, however, he protects the deer, the aggression of the wolves will be turned against him—he destroys the laws of nature and the results affect him directly. The division of the forest into two halves and a corresponding separation of the wolves and the deer can lead to the multiplication of the latter, with all the possible consequences, including the starvation of the former.

The forest ranger can leave the animal world to itself—at best he can frighten away the wolves or shoot the more aggressive ones to show who really rules the forest and protect the deer against eventual extinction. A new species could also appear, hostile toward the wolves and neutral toward the deer, which would assist or replace the forest ranger in his work. As a rule it is nature itself that brings the new species into being, calling upon the wisdom of ecological equilibrium.

This ecological model, though not entirely transferable to the prison reality, illustrates a certain contradiction between the natural laws of life and the planned attempt at their artificial regulation. Finally, it appears that the planned order is unachievable, and itself becomes part of the situation and subject to the same laws. The project's authors and their actions become elements of the situation, and only a wiser or more foolish performance allows that it will influence other elements with a better or worse effect. Their elimination or the establishment of exclusively one's own laws, is impossible. One cannot remove oneself from the situation, since one is always ultimately reduced to one of its components.

In this way the functionaries can influence what is happening between the "people" and the "suckers," but they cannot eliminate these divisions. A new element in this situation could appear—the "fests," who will facilitate steering the community for the administration. Nonetheless, it was not the community which created this element but the need of the given moment. With regard to the administration, we can speak only about a suitable policy toward those groups which enables the administration to retain influence and to control the situation in the institution. The moment the "fests" appear, control becomes easier due to the "divide and conquer" principle.

II. In institution B we are dealing with another type of situation. Here the administration is faced with the problem not of second authority in the prison but with the complete subordination and exploitation of the inmates—achieving complete submission. The way to accomplish this is through breaking down the prisoners' resistance, training them to be obedient and productive.

The response of the inmates is an apparent subjection to those operations. This subordination and least possible resistance occur when the guards and other functionaries violate regulations. The temptation of total power exceeds the legally permissible limits. The prisoner is used to make money; he can be exploited and ill treated in order to demonstrate power over him. At this moment the functionary's authority exceeds its defined boundaries and becomes personal, private dominance. The functionary goes from the role of a supervisor to that of the master and ruler who decides the fate of the slave. By accepting his demands, the prisoners break the rules as well, but only the functionary can be the judge.

Institution B is characterized by a specific hypocrisy. The prisoners are punished for illicit production, having money, theft of tools, making tea, and so on. But it is obvious that the inmate made things for someone, stole the tools for someone, got the tea from someone. The articles they made are not needed by any of the inmates, the stolen tools cannot be used in prison, and the tea was not bought in town by the prisoner. There has to be someone else, and that could only mean the employee of the administration. But the inmates are penalized and the others are ignored. Formally, a certain phenomenon is being combated but, and here lies the hypocrisy, it is being fought by one of the actual perpetrators.

This breach of ethics offers the functionaries a feeling of special omnipotence. They institute prohibitions, seek the offenders, and administer penalties, but despite their participation, they are never involved. They are above it, and they demonstrate this power to the prisoners, intensifying the latter's helplessness.

Select punishment of prisoners for the aforementioned misdemeanors plays not only the role of a fig leaf but also is intended to show the prisoners that blackmail is impossible—the inmates are unable to use the facts against the functionaries; they must remain satisfied with the profits. Actually, the inmates do profit, and those who cannot or do not permit themselves to be exploited find themselves in a worse situation and agree to this imposed symbiosis. The choice which they must make is either to allow themselves to be exploited or to become the object of aggression.

III. In institution C, where strict surveillance of the inmates is impossible, discipline is more flexible. This is favorable for the prisoners since they control themselves and are careful not to cross the boundary beyond which the dissatisfaction of the civil environment would result in repressions on the part of the administration. The administration does not intervene sufficiently in matters concerning the prisoners to arouse their discontent which, transferred to the workplace, could compel the administration to remove the inmates from production and would make it impossible to accomplish the tasks of the institution and reap the profits associated with the exploitation of inmates' labor for private purposes.

The relations described above between the prisoners and the functionaries are, therefore, quite different in the three institutions examined. They are directly dependent on the configurations of relations among the prisoners in institutions A, B, and C which, as we recall, varied as a result of the economic organization of the prisons.

The differentiation of the picture of "hidden life" which is composed of three groups of relations—among the inmates, between the inmates and the functionaries, and among the functionaries—is an outgrowth of the divergent organization of the penal institutions. I have shown this using the example of the first two groups of relations. In the following chapter I shall do so for the third group.

8.

Among the "Screws"

Divisions between Departments of the Prison Staff

The employees of particular departments of the prison staff differ with regard to their opinions concerning the treatment of the convicts.[1]

Functionaries of the security department believe that their most important obligation is surveillance of prisoners' conduct and the execution of discipline and order, while the most important task of the prison is to isolate the prisoners and guarantee security in the prison area. The actions of the entire administration should be carried out with these goals in mind. From this point of view the security staff controls the work of the remaining employees of the penal system.

The functionaries of the economic department and of the department of records and housing maintain that the fundamental task of the penitentiary is to "drive the crooks to work." The work carried out by the administration should concentrate on the organization of the prisoners' work, its ultimate execution, and the organization of the daily schedule, as well as any indispensable support activities.

According to the penitentiary department, the basic premise of the penal institution is the education of the inmates, and the whole organization of the work performed by the prison administration should aim toward this goal.

The differentiation of functions fulfilled by particular departments of the prison staff influences the opinion of their employees regarding the prison's mission and has an impact on the relations between employees of various departments. Each of the departments would like to impose its "philosophy" of executing the court sentences upon the other departments.

In the workplace, close relationships develop among the staff within specific departments. Social life is therefore mainly within particular departments, intensifying in this way their mutual isolation. This situation takes place predominantly in institution A.

Relations between the employees of the security and the penitentiary departments were dominated primarily by animosity. The guards' control over the behavior of the prisoners also includes the relations between inmates and functionaries as well as among the functionaries themselves—mainly those working with prisoners. Hence the functionaries of the penitentiary department are subjects under surveillance by the "security men."

"The security men" claim that the counselors "do nothing, that their work is not real work" and that their behavior toward the inmates is not severe enough. In turn, the counselors believe that they are better educated and consider "the security men" a "bunch of fools." Moreover, they maintain that the "security men" are favored in terms of promotion to higher ranks or posts and receiving more and higher bonuses. The "security men control everybody else, and no one controls them," say the counselors. If the "prisoners are allowed more freedom because they then feel better and are calmer," the "security men" accuse the counselors of neglecting order and discipline, doing nothing, and allowing the development of "hidden life"; in the opinion of the "security men," this is sheer laziness on the part of the counselors and not a didactic method.

The members of the security department are accused of wanting to transform the counselors into an extension of their own functions—they want the counselors to fulfill the same functions. In other words, the counselors maintain, "they would like to have their jobs done for them." In turn, the security department believes that not working with the prisoners and loss of control over them cause problems (self-inflicted injuries, harassment of other inmates, hunger strikes, escapes, etc.) with which they then have to cope. The employees of the other services claim the "security men" do not have to constantly "keep watch," and it is on "our watchfulness in the prison and outside the institution that all security depends—if I don't take notice, then the crooks will think something up, run away. . . ."

The staff members in these departments are aware of their mutual antipathies. Both groups take care to behave well in front of each other—the position of the counselors in this game is weaker. Their behavior is delineated by the way of thinking which compels them to do just so much, and in such a way, as not to provide pretexts for accusations of dereliction of duty. Each initiative and involvement means only an increased number of activities, each of which could be judged as a breach of regulations—and a reason for another functionary or an inmate to inform on them.

In order to prove that they are working, "security men" must register such infringements, as well as in order to have arguments in case of a prisoners' riot—to be able to shift the guilt to the penitentiary department.

The community of the functionaries is divided by antipathies resulting from which of the various departments they belong to, and fear of closer contacts with other staff members, since penetration into internal affairs could prove to be dangerous. It remains, however, a community integrated by its opposition to the inmates.

The functionaries do not maintain friendly relations with the prisoners. They never shake their hands, and they always retain a distinct distance. Neither do they undermine other functionaries' decisions regarding prisoners, nor do they usually accept prisoners' complaints about other functionaries. Any exceptions to these principles are frowned upon by the staff community.

"Screws" with and without Contact with the Prisoners

The largest group on the prison staff includes the functionaries of the security and command department, then those of the economic and financial departments and the department of records and employment, while the smallest group consists of employees of the penitentiary department.[2]

The functionaries of the security department work in guardrooms next to the main gate and by the entrances to the institution, in watch towers on the walls of the prison, in the prisoners' quarters (where the so-called head guards are also employed), and in the inmates' places of work and study; all these posts are, as a rule, filled by junior officers. The functionaries from the department work in twenty-four-hour shifts. Each of the pavilions housing the inmates has its own commander who is an officer of the security department, responsible for discipline and security.

The penitentiary department consists of the counselors (and the head of the department) who work in the inmates' quarters in two daytime shifts. At night only the guards remain with the prisoners.

Functionaries of the economic and financial departments and the departments of records and employment manage the economic infrastructure of the penal institution. They occupy offices in the building of the prison administration, mess-hall, storerooms, and other places connected with the distribution of goods in the institution.

A special group of workers comes from the outside. They include teachers in the prison school and the foremen and manager of the prison workshops. Sometimes, this is an extra part-time job.

Generally speaking, the two groups of employees of the prison system can be distinguished according to their place of work: those who have permanent and direct contact with the inmates; and those whose contact with the inmates is rare, unsystematic, and circumstantial.

Of course, this division is not strictly defined. For example, the administration employs prisoners as office help. This contact, however, is rather irregular (there is not always work for the inmates), and as a rule it involves groups of a few inmates scattered in various rooms. In the aforementioned division, we are concerned with the absence of regular contact with a large group of prisoners, to which the functionaries, as a result of their duties, are formally obliged.

Regular contact with prisoners is maintained predominantly by the counselors and by some of the "security" employees: the guards in the inmates' quarters, the functionaries who guard the prisoners in places of work and study. Regular contact with the inmates is also maintained by the "outside" workers: the teachers and the foremen.

With the exception of the management, the middle and lower personnel regard work with the prisoners as attractive. For example, the dismissal of a staff member from work with the inmates and his transference to another post is considered a penalty. Work involving contact with the prisoners is particularly attractive in institution B. It is less monotonous and offers opportunities for additional illegal earnings and for obtaining various goods via the inmates—as I described in chapter 7.

But the profits which could be made from working with the inmates can result not only from their direct exploitation but also from the appropriation and removal from the institution of various articles (tools, raw materials, paint, work clothes, etc.) whose disappearance is regarded as theft or destruction committed by the prisoners. An example was the disappearance from institution B of a considerable amount of sand and cement which was officially explained as a sign of the protest of the inmates against a further expansion of the institution buildings: for a period of time the inmates filled their pockets with the sand and cement and then scattered and trampled the material into the ground.

If the functionaries who work with the inmates "stick together" and jointly settle all sorts of business deals, then those who have no such opportunities are jealous and happy to learn about those getting caught taking advantage of their position. The "security" functionaries who belong to the "non-contact" group and the management of the institution try to keep surveillance over this process and act on visible manifestations of its existence: Functionary Z was caught drinking vodka bought with money extorted from an inmate in return for annulling a report (which was intended as punishment for an insult—a false report). As a result he was "moved up"—to the watchtower (the "cockerel"). Another functionary sold a meat chopper to an acquaintance in the nearby town. The buyer showed it off to a neighbor who liked it so much that she asked where she could buy one. Having found out that similar articles are made by the inmates and can be bought cheaply, she telephoned a friend who worked in the penal institution. This friend happened to be the head of the penitentiary department who wanted to know the source of information and the identity of the "peddler." The unlucky functionary of the security department was interviewed, confronted with the purchaser, and punished by being "moved up." These examples show, among other things, the reason why work with the inmates is more attractive than those posts where such contacts are limited.

The income made by the functionaries off the prisoners is extra, and not controlled by families and wives. By offering vodka and delivering various articles, the inmates corrupt the employees responsible for surveillance in the institution; the latter also profit by shutting their eyes to the flourishing business. After all, sometimes even the management of the institution "needs something"; believing it inappropriate to negotiate directly with the prisoners, they use an intermediary from among the lower personnel.

The struggle of the governing body of the institution with the corruption of the functionaries is unsuccessful in the long run. It only produces anger on the part of the personnel, who, as a result of the special way in which they execute their duties and playing off the mistaken decisions of the highest officials, can contribute to an increased discontent among the inmates: riots, self-inflicted injuries, hunger strikes, fights, production strikes, etc., all of which indicate to the superior authorities the faulty work of the prison management. Therefore, the prison management must make concessions to lower personnel, or otherwise it opens itself up to the risk of further trouble—a negative estimation of its work. These concessions are the reason why even the highest officials participate indirectly in the illegal operations of the lower personnel and sustain the division into the privileged functionaries who enjoy "contact" with the inmates and those "without contact."

Inside and Outside the Prison Walls

In institution C, as we already know, the majority of the prisoners are employed outside the prison and escorted by specially chosen groups of functionaries from the security department (personnel is rotated for this duty). Those staff members who remain in the institution control a smaller group of inmates who are employed there or attend school.

In reality, the functionaries are scattered within the institution and even more so when directed to various places outside the institution. This is why the number of contacts made by the staff in institution C, in time and space, is much smaller than in the previous two examples. Also the degree of menace contained in contacts in institutions A and B is less in institution C. Social contacts are determined to a lesser extent by membership in the same departments or by contact, or the lack thereof, with the convicts.

Responsibility for the inmates lies heaviest with those who supervise the prisoners outside the prison. If no trouble is noted, then everything is in order. The methods used to achieve this state of affairs are the concern of the functionaries, although it is known that prisoner-informers note their behavior outside the institution.

The management of the establishment does not take advantage of information about functionaries' misconduct (such as leaving the workplace, drinking alcohol with the inmates) until faulty supervision or close contacts with the inmates become a source of problems, for example, come to the attention of the civil workers who might relay the information to the higher authorities of the institution.

The fact that the inmates are often exploited by the highest functionaries for their own private purposes is, after all, observed by the personnel supervising the prisoners; this is why it is better not to have the staff as an enemy.

The fundamental principle in contacts between the functionaries in this institution is not to "interfere" without reason—or at least not as long as everything is going well.

The relationships between the functionaries, as outlined above, show that the organization of the penal institutions is also important for this group. In institution A they are determined by affiliation to one of the departments of the prison staff, in institution B by work with or without contact with the inmates, and in institution C by the scattered workplaces.

I must add, however, that I examined this group in less depth, partly because the functionaries were only in the prison for certain periods at a time—after all, a larger part of the day and night is spent outside the penal institution, at home. Moreover, the functionaries were unwilling to talk about their work, for fear of disclosing information about their relations within the prison, and also because of their dissatisfaction on the job.

Standard interviews conducted at the end of 1979 by a member of the prison staff with twenty guards and twenty counselors show that in their opinion the work of the functionaries is underestimated by society and that they set their profession at the very bottom of the hierarchy of professional prestige. Half of them also felt isolated within the community of the functionaries.

In characterizing the negative phenomena of their profession, the respondents mentioned as the most important: the stifling of criticism, the poor work of some of the functionaries, their passivity and indifference as well as the prevalence of favoritism, cliques, drunkenness, gossip, informing, lack of concern for the working man. Promotion among the prison staff, in their opinion, was guaranteed by the ability to make a good impression on one's superior and mutual support, and to a very small extent on professional skills and hard work.

The relationship between the security department and the penitentiary department were described by the persons interviewed as conflicting, and they often saw no any positive aspects in the work of the other department.[3]

Outside their places of work, the functionaries avoid mutual encounters and even in work would gladly ignore each other.

9.

Social Relations in "Hidden Life"

The Model Thesis and the Reality of the Penal Institution

The fundamental principle of the penal institution is control which permeates all aspects of the life of the subordinates. Achieving this kind of control is possible only in isolation from the external world. Its substance is a special mode of organizing the life of the convicts. This pattern, which defines the course of the daily routine of the subordinates, is repeated in endless continua of consecutive days. It also expresses the special position chosen by the designers of totalitarian institutions in relation to the subordinates. By placing themselves above them and the life outlined for them, the designers remain as if creators.

The inmate's life is supposed to be a duplication of the life enjoyed by free people: each person must work and learn and have leisure time and rest, while food, clothing, and articles of personal use (hygiene) must be guaranteed for him or her. Everyone receives the same things in the same amounts—complete standardization and uniformity.

The behavior of the subordinates is controlled as well. The place and activities of each subordinate are strictly fixed for each day and within the space of a closed area. Consecutive days are copies of the previously established schedule of a previous day. A week, a month, a year, or a decade are like books of various thickness, each with identical pages.

The pattern of social relations is fixed as well. By foreseeing the possibility of unexpected situations, those carrying out prison life—supervisors—are endowed with the competencies of rule maker, judge, and executioner.

Prisons seem to personify a model of righteousness and social order—an adaptation to the rules makes free will useless. The subordinates are ordered to relinquish responsibility, which is taken over by the institution. They are compressed into a "matrix" of life, and this is the primary purpose of the penal system.

So much for the idealized concept of the prison institution. In practice, it turns out that people are unable to find their place in this artificial life, and they deviate from the strictly delineated paths of conduct. Fearing punishment, they conceal their misconduct from the supervisors. The organization of life in prison is the reason why illegal action is often committed in full view of other people. But the others commit offenses as well. Everyone, therefore, witnesses misconduct and can testify against each other. This mutuality serves as a guarantee against disclosure. When everyone can become the accused there is no accuser—this is, already, qualitatively a totally different situation from the planned one. It signifies a threat of compromising the very foundation of the totalitarian institution, the authority of its designers and executors. Therefore, no such disclosure is permitted. But by keeping this type of a secret the supervisors lose their moral purity—it becomes impossible to retain the clear-cut form of conduct in the totalitarian institution, and now they too must conceal the fact that they are aware of this state of affairs. They are no longer the personification of righteousness. This "original sin" deprives them of authority in the eyes of the subordinates. They deceive themselves that in intensifying control they will be able to restore the postulated state of affairs. The system of informing grows and increases uncertainty in mutual contacts. The supervisors count on the fact that the subordinates by themselves will begin to control their own behavior in the presence of others. But by doing so, they recognize their subjectivity. It is in this subjectivity that the subordinates discover a way to reduce doubts about their own solidarity.

The supervisors reach for measures contrary to the rule-of-law proclaimed by them and do so ineffectively. After all, it is enough for them that the subordinates just play the desired roles of behavior in their presence.

Reducing supervisors to the level of lawlessness is a success for the subordinates. Both sides know that they are not acting "within the law," but the circumstances demand from them that they act according to formal models. Besides these, in situations which they have defined as having never existed, a new life emerges which they regulate themselves in a specific way and which becomes a truly "hidden life" of the prison.

The prison institution no longer dreams about the elimination of "hidden life" but is only left with choosing what attitude to have toward it. The supervisors who were supposed to control the situation became one of its elements. From a position in which it was intended that they watch over processes developing in the prison, they were reduced to one of the elements of this process, and this dissolved the artificiality of institution life.[1]

The Economic Organization and Social Structure of the Prison

"Hidden life" in prison is comprised of three types of relationships: among the subordinates, between the subordinates and the supervisors, and among the supervisors. The material I have presented shows that in the three different types of penal institutions, these relationships differ. My research has also changed the picture of these relationships from that which has been noted in correctional institutions until now.

In previous models of relationships within the "hidden life" of the prison, it was said that the exploitation of some of the inmates by others resulted in two distinct groups: the exploiters and the exploited, as well as a normative system which constitutes this division. In this way, a specific organization of inmates emerged which concentrated on controlling the functionaries. The word *control* should be stressed, since attempts at its elimination failed. I have also shown that as a consequence of processes within the community of institution A, yet another version of the organizational structure of the prisoners has become possible, although its essence remains the same as the one outlined above.

Relations between the functionaries are delineated by their affiliation to a specific type of service (department), each of which fulfills a different function in the prison. A struggle for status in the institution integrates the interests of their own departments and breeds distrust in relations with employees of other departments.

In institution B where there were possibilities for obtaining goods not by the exploitation of another prisoner but in cooperation with him—by means of illicit production and trade—the relations in the prison community were shaped differently than in institution A. Production and trade created an illegal market, and the latter generated and guided processes within that community.

The existence of an illegal market is possible above all because of the participation of the functionaries, who created the demand. They also sell the products cheaply, and profits from passing illegal correspondence, etc. undoubtedly benefit them. An insurance against interference by those functionaries who do not take part in the transactions is the corruption of the latter by colleagues involved in the illegal traffic.

In a semi-open institution, such as institution C, the inmates enjoy a decidedly broader contact with the outside world and are not forced to obtain goods by means of the exploitation of another inmate or cooperation with him—they remain independent. As long as the prisoners are permitted to retain this state of affairs, they generally meet the expectations of the functionaries and, apart from fulfilling their official tasks, allow themselves to be exploited for administration workers' private deals.

If this arrangement works without serious disturbances, mobilization of the staff is unnecessary; it suffices that they fulfill a minimum of imposed duties. This state of affairs, as well as the fact that workplaces are in scattered locations, contributes to the reason why relations between them are less cohesive than in the other two institutions.

Various models of interpersonal relations in the three institutions examined seem to depend on the specific situation which each one of them creates.

The basic determinant for relations in the institution seems to lie within the community of the prisoners. The structure of the prison community and its functions are conditioned by access to consumer goods and the cooperative or noncooperative way of obtaining them (via exploitation of someone else or independently). The character of those variables is delineated by the degree of isolation (the type of the institution: closed, semi-open) and the type of production in which the prisoners are employed and on which the possibility and scale of the illegal production and trade depend.[2]

It could be said, therefore, that relations governing the "hidden life" of the prison are a function of its economic organization and that by knowing the elements of this organization one can predict an approximate model of relations in the "hidden life" of a given penitentiary.

It is difficult to say whether the economic organization has such an essential impact on "hidden life" in prisons in other countries as it does in Polish penal institutions. The pauperization of the inmates may not necessarily resemble that prevalent in Polish prisons in all the institutions of this type. The outcome of my study, however, seems to argue that the relations in the "hidden life" of the prison are always considerably influenced by their specific conditions and that the representation of those relations in all types of penal institutions cannot be reduced to a common denominator—just as it is impossible to do so for the prisons in a single country.

The findings of this study accentuate the importance of the active role played by the behavior of individuals in constructing a social reality. The individuals, by seeking and penetrating the situation from the point of view of the measures which best meet their requirements, enter into interactions whose regular patterns constitute a social structure.[3] At the same time, it should be stressed that the condition for the existence of such interactions need not be the goals shared by the individuals but the significance they employ and which make an agreement possible. People can unite not necessarily only to achieve common goals; having different aims, they might need each other and cooperate to accomplish their own separate purposes.[4]

The social structure in this interpretation is therefore a configuration of mutually connected events that, by repeating themselves, bring to an end and reset into motion a series of social actions. The social structure is created by events rather than by things and thus the concept of the structure is more dynamic than static.[5]

If we introduce changes into a penal institution that in a substantial way define the range and manner of obtaining consumer goods, then the inmates and the functionaries will strive toward undertaking such interpersonal relations which will make it possible to attain optimum profits in the new situation. They will hold on to certain old models of interaction as long as they remain functional. This appears to explain why in different penal institutions we can come across similar and different elements within the informal structures of the prison communities.

Notes

Introduction

1. When conducting commissioned research or as an assistant of a Student Penitentiary Group in 1976-83, I visited 13 penal institutions including those in Iława, Czarne, Fordon, Łodz (Sikawa), Goleniow, Nowogard, Uherce, Łupkow, and Moszczaniec (these three in the Bieszczady region), Lubliniec, Sieradz, Mielecin, and Słuzewiec (Warsaw), and three reformatories in Warsaw, Białystok, and Malbork.

1. A Reserved Terrain

1. See E. Goffman, *Asylums* (Harmondsworth: Penguin, 1976), and M. Foucault, *Discipline and Punish: The Birth of the Prison* (New York: Vintage, 1979).
2. See P. Moczydłowski and A. Rzeplinski, "Group Protests in Penal Institutions: The Polish Case," *Howard Journal of Criminal Justice* 24, no. 1, pp. 10-19.
3. "The functionary is obliged to keep secret all issues with which he became acquainted indirectly or directly in connection with the performance of official duties, if those issues have been recognized as secret or if their secrecy is demanded by public welfare or official reasons. . . . The obligation to keep the secret is maintained both during work and after discharge. . . . The Minister of Justice or a superior authorized by him can release the functionary from the duty of keeping the secret in certain instances." From article 24 of the law concerning prison staffs issued Dec. 10, 1959; see *Dziennik Ustaw PRL* (hereafter *Dz. U.*) [Government Regulations and Law Gazette of the Polish People's Republic], Warsaw, May 31, 1984, no. 2.
4. Concerning the size of the prison population in Poland, for instance, the prison functionaries were aware of it and protested against this state of affairs in 1981; see Moczydłowski and Rzeplinski, "Protesty zbiorowe w zakładach karnych" [Group protests in penal institutions] typescript, 1982, library of the Institute of Social Prevention and Resocialization, Warsaw University (hereafter IPSiR, UW).
5. The political functions of prisons are discussed by D. Daffe in *Correctional Policy and Prison Organization* (New York: The Free Press, 1975), and D. Katz and R. L. Kahn, *Społeczna psychologia organizacji* [The social psychology of organization] (Warsaw: PWN, 1979).
6. Foucault also treats the prison as an instrument in governing: "the prison transformed the punitive procedure into a penitentiary technique; the careful archipelago transported this technique from the penal institution to the entire social body" (*Discipline and Punish*, p. 298).
7. See Katz and Kahn, *Społeczna psychologia*, p. 178.

8. T. Szymanowski, "Udział społeczenstwa w wykonaniu kary pozbawienia wolnosci w Polsce po II wojnie swiatowej" [The participation of society in the execution of a sentence of imprisonment in Poland after World War II] in *Spory wokoł reformy wieziennictwa* [Debates concerning the reform of the penal system], S. Walczak, ed. (Warsaw: IPSiR UW, 1985), pp. 127-52.

9. R. Merton, *Social Theory and Social Structure* (Glencoe, Ill.: The Free Press, 1949), p. 303.

10. Ibid.

11. In Poland the Central Administration of Penal Institutions in the Department of Justice initiated numerous closed symposia and conferences on the prison system, with the participation of authorities and academic scholars. For example, a symposium on "Negative Symptoms of Prison Subculture—Measures and Methods of Counteraction" was organized by the Central Administration and held in Popowo in December 1974. Material from the symposium was published under the same title by the Central Administration in April 1975. An ideological conference of high-level personnel took place Feb. 24-26, 1983, also in Popowo. Material from this conference, issued by the Central Administration, also contained an analysis of the situation in the prison system.

12. The Institute of Research into Court Law, for example, is part of the Department of Justice. In ruling no. 73 of the Chairman of the Council of Ministers [Zarzadzenie Prezesa Rady Ministrow], Sept. 28, 1973, concerning the establishment of the institute, which was formed as a result of a transformation of the Center of Research into Criminality, we read: "§3. Control over the institute is kept by the minister of justice. . . . §5. The detailed range of the activity of the institute and the range and method of activity of its organs are delineated by a statute given by the minister of justice. . . . §6. The organizational structure is defined by the minister of justice." In a ruling of the Minister of Justice of Oct. 31, 1973, concerning the statute and organizational structure of the institute, we read: "§16.2. Suitable posts in the institute can be filled by employees of other organizational units of the department with the retention of the heretofore mentioned rights." In practice this meant that employees of the prison system were employed as scientific workers of the institute. Moreover, the Central Administration employed all the workers of certain departments of the institute, who retained all privileges: ranks in prison staff, wages, etc. Paragraph 4 of the ruling states: "Personnel questions of the institute are managed by the personnel department of the Ministry of Justice. . . ."

13. Ruling no. 73 of the Chairman of the Council of Ministers says: "§4. The purpose of the institute is to organize and conduct scientific research regarding the efficacy of measures applied by the courts and the regularities of their execution." Students and workers of the Institute of Social Prevention and Resocialization of Warsaw University were turned down by the Central Administration in connection with research they wanted to carry out in penal institutions.

14. That the prison system is an organization with monopolistic ambitions is emphasized by Katz and Kahn, *Społeczna psychologia*. See also P. Moczydłowski and A. Rzeplinski, "Warunki i problemy resocjalizacji wiezniow pracujacych jako robotnicy w zakładach karnych w Polsce w latach 70-tych" [Conditions and problems of the resocialization of inmates employed as workers in penal institutions in

Poland during the 1970s] in *Problemy patologii i przestepczosci* [Problems of pathology and criminality], ed. A. Wojcik (Warsaw: ANS, 1985), pp. 456-523.

15. A list of such prohibitions was formulated by the prison system in reply to a request by an academic investigator concerning permission to undertake research in penal institutions.

16. See K. R. Popper, *Open Society and Its Enemies*, vol. 2 (London: Compton Printing, 1974), pp. 212-23.

17. Merton writes: "In the totalitarian society, the centralization of institutional control is a source of opposition to science; in other structures, the extension of scientific research is of greater importance. Dictatorship organizes, centralizes and hence intensifies sources of resistance against science which in a liberal structure remain unorganized, diffuse and often latent" (*Social Theory*, p. 303).

2. Prison Paranoia

1. See the law on prison staffs issued Dec. 10, 1959, articles 2 and 10. The legal foundations of the organization of this service are provided above all by that law; by ruling no. 52/82, Oct. 10, 1982, of the Central Administration of Penal Institutions of the Department of Justice [Ustawa o Sluzbie Wieziennej CZZK Ministra Sprawiedliwosci] concerning the organizational structure and tasks of the regional administration of penal institutions and detention centers; and by the ruling of Nov. 4, 1982, of the director of the Central Administration on establishing the detailed range of activities for organizational units and posts in the regional administration of penal institutions and organizational units in detention and penal institutions. The 1982 documents were never published and unfortunately remain mostly secret; legal publications contain only small excerpts. In preparing this chapter I based my statements both on published sources and on information I collected myself.

2. See excerpts of ruling no. 52/82 in *Wybor tekstow zrodlowych do nauki prawa karnego i wykonawczego* [Select source material for the study of executive penal law], ed. S. Lelental (Lodz: UL, 1984), pp. 87-92.

3. See excerpts of ruling no. 6/82 in *Wybor tekstow zrodlowych*, pp. 93-99.

4. See excerpts of ruling no. 52/82 in *Wybor tekstow zrodlowych*, pp. 87-92.

5. M. Porowski, "Funkcje administracji penitencjarnej" [Functions of the penitentiary administration], in *Problemy wspolczesnej penitencjarystyki w Polsce* [Problems of contemporary penitentiaries in Poland] (Warsaw: Wydaw. Praw., 1984), pp. 138-51.

6. Ibid.

7. Ibid.

8. See Moczydlowski and Rzeplinski, "Warunki i problemy"; Porowski, "Funkcje"; and *Praca skazanych odbywajacych kare pozbawienia wolnosci* [The work of convicts in confinement], ed. T. Bojarski, Z. Holda, and J. Baranowski (Lublin: UMCS, 1985).

9. See excerpts of ruling no. 6/82 in *Wybor tekstow zrodlowych*, pp. 87-92, and Porowski, "Funkcje."

10. Porowski, "Funkcje," p. 150.

11. See Moczydłowski and Rzeplinski, "Warunki i problemy," and Porowski, "Funkcje."

12. Cf. M. Porowski, "Administracja penitencjarna: Zasady organizacji i kierowania" [Penitentiary administration: Principles of organization and management], in *Studia Kryminologiczne, Kryminalistyczne i Penitencjarne* [Criminological, criminalistic and penitentiary studies], vol. 9 (Warsaw, 1979), pp. 339-61. See also Ruling of the Minister of Justice [Zarzadzanie Ministra Sprawiedliwosci], 12 May 1981, concerning the performance and course of service and certain rights and duties of the functionaries of the prison staff in *Dziennik Urzedowy Ministra Sprawiedliwosci* (hereafter *Dz. U. M. S.*) [Regulations gazette of the ministry of justice], 13 July 1981, no. 3, item 14, and the ruling of the Minister of Justice, 28 Sept. 1981, concerning the establishment of the rights of superiors in certain issues of the functionaries of the prison staff, in *Dz. U. M. S.*, Warsaw, 30 Nov. 1981, no. 5, item 30; and the cited ruling no. 52/82 of the Minister of Justice and ruling no. 6/82 of the Director of the Central Administration of the Penal Institutions. This problem is discussed more extensively in chapter 3.

13. Cf. S. Walczak, *Prawo penitencjarne. Zarys systemu* [Penitentiary law: An outline of a system] (Warsaw: PWN, 1972), p. 222.

14. J. Zieleniewski understands the duty to mean such an activity on the part of a member of an institution "so that certain things at certain moments would find themselves in a state defined by a moral, legal, customary, or conventional norm or in a state indicated by the director of an ensemble authorized to issue such directives," cf. J. Zieleniewski, *Organizacja i zarzadzanie* [Organization and management] (Warsaw: PWN, 1979), p. 402.

15. Cf. M. Porowski, "Administracja penitencjarna," p. 358.

16. *Kodeks Karny Wykonawczy* (henceforth *KKW*) [Executive penal code, article 38, para. 2].

17. M. Porowski, "Administracja penitencjarna," pp. 358-59.

18. This excerpt is from the work by Z. Karl, "Krotki zarys struktury organizacijnej polskiego systemu wieziennego w latach 1944-56" [A brief outline of the organizational structure of the Polish penal system in the years 1944-1956], *Przeglad Wieziennictwa*, no. 2/17 (Warsaw, 1962), pp. 3, 4, 5. It concerns the establishment of the duties of a governor of a penal institution according to an instruction concerning the prison regulations, issued on 11 June 1945. See Karl, "Krotki zarys," p. 42. Considering the difficult access to various regulations, which are sometimes secret or intended for internal use only, the range of the duties is illustrated by available material. Eventual divergencies with the present-day state are not significant enough to distort the ideas contained in my study.

19. For the range of duties belonging to various directors, see Karl, "Krotki zarys," pp. 42-44; the unpublished regulation issued by the Minister of Justice on 1 Oct. 1982; and regulation no. 6/82 of the Director of the Central Administration of the Penal Institutions, of 4 Nov. 1982.

20. Karl, "Krotki zarys," pp. 44-51.

21. See the regulations concerning the range and organization of penitentiary work in penal institutions and detention centers issued by the Ministry of Justice, Central Administration of Penal Institutions, Warsaw, 1977, pp. 53-57.

22. I am unable to give sources for these regulations. The effect of their impact is shown, however, by Moczydłowski and Rzeplinski, "Warunki i problemy": "In the light of the statements of the higher officers of the prison staff one should also negatively estimate the work of the functionaries. In the 1975-1978 period, 22.9 percent of the newly employed junior officers were fired. Of this number, 11 percent were dismissed for disciplinary reasons, while 28 percent left of their own will. In the same period, 31.2 percent of the newly admitted functionaries were punished for misconduct. Abuse of alcohol during work was an easily discernible phenomenon . . . together with the mutual corruption of the functionaries and the inmates and the exploitation of the convicts for the personal purposes of the officers. In 1979, cases of serious disciplinary misdeeds committed by the functionaries were considered by the administration of the prison as rather numerous, although less so than a year earlier" (p. 472).

23. Karl, "Krotki zarys," pp. 30-31.

24. Goffman, *Asylums*, pp. 15-21.

25. Among the postulates of the prisoners protesting in 1981, "a large group of the postulates of the prisoners directly concerned the functionaries of the prison staff. The inmates demanded: the calling to account of the functionaries of the prison staff who (a) are guilty of beating the prisoners, of hanging them by their limbs on barred windows and of applying various forms of pressure, (b) force the inmates to make false statements by the application of various forms of pressure, (c) employ prisoners on their own private property and animal farms for construction work, (d) are guilty of wastefulness and the theft of prisoners' possessions or state property, (e) are guilty of active assault toward passive prisoners . . . ," Moczydłowski and Rzeplinski, "Warunki i problemy," pp. 518-19.

26. D. Kalinich, *The Inmate Economy* (Toronto: D.C. Heath, 1980), p. 7, draws attention to a similar state in prisons in Canada and calls it prison paranoia: "No one totally trusts anyone else and a total stranger is not trusted at all."

27. See G. H. Mead, *Mind, Self and Society* (Chicago: University of Chicago Press, 1934), pp. 212-26 (Polish edition).

28. E. H. Sutherland describes one technique of theft committed by professional burglars in which they involve the victim in illegal deals and then steal from him. The participation of the victim in the illicit deals protects the perpetrators from the victim's notifying the police. See Sutherland, "Behavior System in Crimes," in *Subcultures*, ed. David O. Arnold (Berkeley, Calif.: Glendessary Press, 1973), pp. 9-20.

29. See E. Mokrzycki, *Założenia socjologii humanistycznej* [Premises of humanistic sociology] (Warsaw: PWN, 1971), p. 33, and J. Habermas, *Teoria i praktyka* [Theory and practice] (Warsaw: PWN, 1983).

30. See G. Simmel, *Sociology* [Polish edition] (Warsaw: PWN, 1975), p. 387.

31. See E. Goffman, *The Presentation of Self in Everyday Life* [copyright 1959, E. Goffman, Polish edition] (Warsaw: PIW, 1981), pp. 54, 59, and 101.

32. See M. A. Simon et al., *Centralization, Decentralization in Organizing the Controllers Department* (New York: Controllership Foundation, 1954), p. 85.

33. See J. Zieleniewski, *Organizacja zespołow ludzkich* [Organization of human ensembles] (Warsaw: PWN, 1978), p. 164.

34. This situation involved workers and students from the Department of Law at the University of Salzburg who visited penal institution L in September 1983.

3. Learning from the Failure of Previous Studies

1. Institution B was closest to this model among those institutions studied. But the essential elements of the particular stages of research occurred in all the institutions which I visited. As a rule, experiences of the prison communities with research and investigators are infrequent or nonexistent.

2. This took place in penal institution A in 1975. The research was conducted by a psychologist from Warsaw University. I was told the story by the functionaries who claimed that they intentionally selected a noisy group of inmates "because he was being very clever about work in a prison and thought that he could deal with the crooks like a counselor."

3. This took place in institution A in January 1976.

4. A worker at Warsaw University who conducted research in institution A in January 1976.

4. To Do the Study in Any Way Possible

1. Mokrzycki, *Założenia*, pp. 90-91.

2. Cf. W. J. Thomas, F. Znaniecki, *Chłop polski w Europie i Ameryce* [The Polish peasant in Europe and America], vol. 1 (Warsaw: LSW, 1976), pp. 43-44.

3. This practice is by no means rare among anthropologists who undertake field work. Robert A. Levine writes: "The scientific investigator unacquainted with anthropology may ask, 'Why not formulate a single hypothesis or a set of hypotheses as precisely as possible before field work?' The usual answer is that the anthropologist planning a field trip is faced with the prospect of making an enormous investment of personal resources in a research setting of which he is likely to be appallingly ignorant beforehand" ("Research in Anthropological Field Work," in *A Handbook of Method in Cultural Anthropology*, ed. R. Narrol and R. Cohen [New York: Columbia University Press, 1973], p. 184).

4. This problem is accentuated by ethnomethodologists; for example, the research conducted by Herold Garfinkel on the passing of sentences by jury in *Studies in Ethnomethodology* (Englewood Cliffs, N.J.: Prentice Hall, 1967), pp. 104-15.

5. Cf. Simmel, *Sociology*, pp. 387-88.

6. Cf. Goffman, *The Presentation*, p. 111.

7. J. Szczepanski, *Elementarne pojecia socjologii* [Elementary conceptions of sociology] (Warsaw: PWN, 1967), p. 124.

8. K. Braun, a psychologist in the prison in Tarnow, describes the circumstances of obtaining information:

The most valuable materials are those which are provided by observing the life of the inmates and by analyzing secret notes and messages. One should add that complete utilization of that material was possible thanks to a cooperation of the Department of Security and the Penitentiary Department. . . . A large number of these messages were supplied by the Security Department. . . . Among the juvenile convicts I obtained most information about the code from the persecuted and victimized inmates, the so-called non-people, who, embittered by the wrongs suffered at the hands of the code-users, provided me with extremely interesting material. This is why former code users, and current non-people, expelled from the code and freed from the compulsion to retain the secret, offered exhaustive data concerning "hidden life" . . . One could also make use of facts supplied by the code users who, caught while committing some offenses in connection with the code, made explanations.

See "Drugie zycie wsrod skazanych młodocianych" [Hidden life among juvenile offenders] in *Negatywne przejawy podkultury: Srodki i sposby przeciwdziałania* [Negative symptoms of prison subculture: Measures and methods of counteraction] (Warsaw: CZZK, 1975), pp. 39-40.

9. Braun also indicates the garrulity of the prisoners. "In conversations with the code users one can utilize their loquacity and readiness to show off. They often involuntarily say more than they would want to say, and the most intelligent among the prisoners can be provoked to talk about the code and during the discussion, by defending their attitude, they unintentionally also provide some facts" (ibid., p. 40).

10. This partly involved eliciting frustration used by the ethnomethodologists in their experiments by undermining the feeling of joint reality, created in the interactions. See Garfinkel, *Studies in Ethnomethodology*, pp. 77-103. I did the same albeit much more delicately, in order not to shatter the interaction with the persons under examination, and only to produce the need to supply me with additional information, to convince me or correct mistaken convictions.

11. Most probably this tendency is produced by the very situation of isolation. The specificity of experiences, the feeling of injustice, the lack of a possibility of their articulation all create a strong state of tension and the need to share one's experiences, for which it is difficult to find a form of expression—the inmates lose their train of thought and say whatever is on their minds at the moment.

12. See M. Ziołkowski, "O czterech mozliwosciach socjologicznego podejscia do zjawisk jezykowych" [On four possibilities of a sociological approach to linguistic phenomena] in *Zagadnienia socjo- i psycholingwistyki* [The problems of socio- and psycholinguistics] (Warsaw: Ossolineum, 1980), p. 153.

13. See J. Gumperz, "The Speech Community," in *Language and Social Context*, ed. P. P. Giglioli (Harmondsworth: Penguin, 1972), p. 225.

14. D. Hymes, "Socjolingwistyka i etnografia mowienia" [Sociolinguistics and the ethnography of speech] in *Jezyk i społeczenstwo* [Language and society] (Warsaw: Czytelnik, 1980), pp. 41-82.

15. B. Gieremek, "O jezykach tajemnych" [On secret languages] in *Teksty* 2/50, 1980, p. 20.

16. See also H. Michalski and J. Morawski, *Słownik gwary wieziennej* [Dictionary of prison argot] (Warsaw: MSW, 1971).

17. Gieremek, "O jezykach tajemnych," p. 26.

18. Cf. I. Kurcz, *Psycholingwistyka* [Psycholinguistics] (Warsaw: PWN, 1976), p. 22.

19. Ibid., pp. 22-23.
20. Ibid., p. 23.
21. J. Kurczewski, "Bluzg, grypserka, 'drugie zycie': interpretacje podkultury" [Curse, code, 'hidden life': Interpretations of a subculture] in *Git ludzie w szkole* [Git people in school], ed. M. Kosewski (Warsaw: UW, 1981), p. 97.
22. For more on this subject, see A. V. Cicourel, "Cognitive-Linguistic Aspects of Social Research," *Sozialwissenschaftliche Annalen*, Band 1 (Vienna: Physica Verlag, 1977), pp. 1-21.
23. The incident took place in institution A.
24. For more on this subject, see Cicourel, "Cognitive-Linguistic Aspects of Social Research"; and Cicourel, *Cognitive Sociology: Language and Meaning in Social Interaction* (New York: The Free Press, 1974), pp. 99-140.
25. Cf. Ziolkowski, *Znaczenie, interakcja, rozumienie* [Significance, interaction, understanding] (Warsaw: PWN, 1981), p. 256.
26. Cicourel, *Cognitive Sociology*, pp. 99-140.
27. Ziolkowski, *Znaczenie*, p. 266. Cf. also Mokrzycki's criticism of the concept of understanding as interpreted by S. Nowak in Mokrzycki, *Zalozenie*, and S. Nowak, *Metodologia badan spolecznych* [Methodology of social research] (Warsaw: PWN, 1985).

5. Prisons Selected for the Study

1. S. Malkowski, "Drugie zycie w zakladzie wychowawczym" [Hidden life in a reformatory] *Etyka*, no. 8 (1971), pp. 135-47; Malkowski, "Cele i wartosci 'Ludzi' " [Goals and values of the "People"] in *Git Ludzie w Szkole*, ed. Kosewski, pp. 27-50; A. Pilinow and J. Wasilewski, "Nieformalna stratyfikacja wychowankow zakladu poprawczego" [Informal stratification of inmates of a correctional institution] *Etyka*, no. 8 (1971), pp. 149-64; S. Jedlewski, *Nieletni w zakladzie poprawczym* [Juveniles in a correctional institution] (Warsaw: Wydaw. Praw., 1972); B. Malak, "Własnosci osobowosci a rodzaj uczestnictwa w podkulturze zakladu poprawczego" [Personality properties and the type of participation in the subculture of a correctional institution] in *Z zagadnien psychologii agresji* [Select problems of the psychology of aggression], ed. A. Fraczek (Warsaw: PIPS, 1975), pp. 201-31; R. L. Drwal, *Osobowosc wychowankow zakladu poprawczego* [The personality of the inmates of reformatories] (Wrocław: Ossolineum, 1981).
2. M. Rydz, "Drugie zycie wiezniow mlodocianych w zakladzie karno-sledczym w X" [Hidden life of juvenile convicts in the penal detention center in X] *Etyka*, no. 8 (1971), pp. 161-75; B. Jarzebowska-Baziak, *Praca wychowawcza w zakladzie karnym dla mlodocianych* [Educational work in a penal institution for juvenile offenders] (Warsaw: Wydaw. Praw., 1972); Braun, *Drugie zycie*.
3. B. Zielinska, "Strategia resocjalizacyjna recydywistow" [The resocialization strategy for recidivists] (MA thesis cited by A. Podgorecki, *Zarys socjologii prawa* [An outline of the sociology of law] [Warsaw: PWN, 1971]); M. Gordon, "Drugie zycie wsrod skazanych doroslych pierwszy raz karanych i recydiwistow" [Hidden life among the adult first offenders and recidivists] in *Negatywne przejawy.*

4. A. Podgorecki, "Drugie zycie: Proba hipotezy wyjasniajacej" [Hidden life: An attempted explanatory hypothesis] *Etyka*, no. 8 (1971), pp. 177-83; J. Kwasniewski, "Koncepcja podkultur dewiacynych" [The conception of deviatory subcultures] in *Zagadnienia patologii spolecznej* [Problems of social pathology], ed. A. Podgorecki (Warsaw: PWN, 1976), pp. 203-41; Kosewski, *Agrsywni przestepcy* [Aggressive criminals] (Warsaw: Wydaw. Praw., 1977); Kurczewski, "Bluzg, grypserka, drugie zycie"; Cz. Czapow, "Style oddziaływania wychowawczego" [Styles of educational influence] in *Socjotechnika: Style działania* [Sociotechnology: Styles of activity], ed. A. Podgorecki (Warsaw: KiW, 1972), pp. 169-212; S. Jedlewski, *Analiza pedagogiczna systemu dyscyplinarno-izolacyjnego w resocjalizacji nieletnich* [A pedagogical analysis of the disciplinary-isolation system in the resocialization of juveniles] (Wrocław: Ossolineum, 1981).

5. See *KKW* [Executive penal code], chapter 9, art. 39, paragraph 1.

6. Cf. S. Walczak, *Prawo penitencjarne w zarysie* [Penitentiary law in an outline] (Warsaw: PWN, 1972), pp. 211-15.

7. Ibid., pp. 215-22.

6. Among "Crooks"

1. Cf. A. Podgorecki, *Zarys socjologii prawa* [An outline of the sociology of law] (Warsaw: PWN, 1971); J. Kwasniewski, "Koncepcja podkultur dewiacyjnych" [The conception of deviatory subcultures] in *Zagadnienia patologii spolecznej* [Problems of social pathology], ed. A. Podgorecki (Warsaw: PWN, 1970), pp. 203-41; M. Los, "Peer Subcultures in Correctional Institutions: Comparative Approach" (typescript in IPSiR, UW); R. Ł. Drwal, *Osobowosc wychowankow zakladow poprawczych* [The personality of the inmates of reformatories] (Wrocław: Ossolineum, 1981), and works cited in note 4 of chapter 5 of this book.

2. This attitude appears to be shared by Maria Łos and Palmer Anderson, who describe "hidden life" in Polish correctional institutions: "The most important part of social life in the correctional institutions for boys is '*grypserka*'—the 'secret code'[my emphasis] which consists of special language and values pertaining to social interaction among 'people' on the one hand, and 'slaves' on the other. Rules concern mainly the 'cursed,' the 'rituals,' the 'oaths' and the 'spying' (denouncing or informing). The rules are particularly important in determining and perpetuating the social division: 'people' and 'slaves' and are very much adhered to in determining the status of a new boy coming to the institution"; see M. Łos and P. Anderson, "The Second Life: A Cross-cultural View of Peer Subcultures in Correctional Institutions" (typescript in IPSiR, UW).

3. M. Łos writes: "According to Polish data, we have the following picture: a very sharp division exists of inmates into the clearly dichotomized, basic categories which in juvenile argot are called 'people' as the dominant caste, and 'slaves' (non-people) referring to the subordinate caste"; see Łos and Anderson, "The Second Life," p. 3.

4. Łos and Anderson write: "The secret life in correctional and treatment institutions in Poland and the United States have much in common. This finding is not surprising as the structural and functional characteristics of these institutions are, to an extent, similar in both countries" (ibid., p. 25); R. Ł. Drwal, *Osobowosc wychowankow*, pp. 13-14.

5. Despite the fact that the "fests" and the "git people" treat the other prisoners as "victims" they distinguish three separate categories: the "Swiss," the typical victims and the "fags." Membership in these groups depends on the way in which an inmate was "victimized."

6. The message does not contain any data which would make it possible to identify the addressee by the administration. The writing and sending of such messages is forbidden.

7. The prison staff does not allow inmates "to be deprived of the code by force" in its presence. It does, however, favor the "victimization" of the "git people"; sometimes, the staff abandon their posts by leaving the "fests" with the "git people" so the former can "decode" the latter.

8. Faience—an illegally produced article, or a constituent part.

9. Cf. G. M. Sykes, *The Society of Captives* (Princeton: Princeton University Press, 1958); G. M. Sykes, "The Pains of Imprisonment," in *The Sociology of Punishment and Correction*, N. B. Johnston et al., eds. (New York: Wiley, 1962), pp. 131-37; Ch. Tittle, "Inmate Organization: Sex Differentiation and the Influence of Criminal Subculture," in *American Sociological Review* 34 (1969), pp. 492-505; A. Etzioni, *A Comparative Analysis of Complex Organizations* (New York: The Free Press, 1975); Podgorecki, "Drugie zycie"; Kurczewski, "Bluzg, grypserka, drugie zycie"; Małkowski, "Drugie zycie"; B. Waligora, *Funkcjonowanie człowieka w warunkach izolacji wieziennej* [The functioning of man in conditions of penal isolation] (Poznan: UAM, 1974); and others.

10. Cf. I Irwin and D. Cressey, "Thieves, Convicts, and the Inmate Culture," *Social Problems*, no. 10 (1970); H. Clines, "The Determinants of Normative Patterns in Correctional Institutions," in *Scandinavian Studies in Criminology* II, ed. N. Christie (Oslo: Oslo University Press, 1968), pp. 173-84; C. Wellford, "Factors Associated with Adoption of the Inmate Code: A Study of Normative Assimilation," *Journal of Criminal Law, Criminology, and Police Science* 58 (June 1967), pp. 197-203; D. Clemmer, *The Prison Community* (Boston: 1940); B. Schwartz, "Pre-institutional vs. Situational Influence in a Correctional Community," *Journal of Criminal Law, Criminology, and Police Science* 63 (1971), pp. 532-42; Ch. W. Thomas, "Theoretical Perspectives on Prisonization: A Comparison of the Importation and Deprivation Modes," *Journal of Criminal Law, Criminology, and Police Science* 68, no. 1 (1977), pp. 135-45; Cz. Czapow, "Style oddziaływania"; Zielinska, "Strategia resocjalizacyjna"; and others.

7. Between the "Screws" and the "Crooks"

1. Cf. works by Sykes, Podgorecki, Małkowski, and others.

2. Cf. E. E. Flyn, "Pattern and Sources of Prison Violence: Implications for a Theory and Control," *Seminaire international sur les Lomgues points d'empris-*

onement (Montreal, 1978), p. 304; P. Wheatley, "Riots and Serious Mass Disorder," *Prison Service Journal* 44 (October 1981), pp. 1-4; P. Moczydłowski and A. Rzeplinski, "Group Protests in Penal Institutions in Poland in 1981" (a research report), Warsaw University, 1982.

3. See also Podgorecki, "Drugie zycie."

4. Sykes, *The Society of Captives.*

5. See B. J. McCarthy, "Keeping an Eye on the Keeper: Prison Corruption and Its Control," *The Prison Journal* 2 (Fall-Winter 1984), pp. 113-25; Kalinich, *The Inmate Economy.*

6. Cf. cited works by Thomas, Czapow, Irwin and Cressey, and Clemmer and other supporters of the importation theory.

7. It appears that certain observed phenomena concerning the attitude of the functionaries to the informal structures ("hidden life") in Polish penal institutions were almost universal. This fact is supported by material from a symposium organized by the Central Administration of Penal Institutions and held in Popowo near Warsaw on December 16-17, 1974. This symposium was devoted to the collection of information on experiences regarding methods of overcoming "hidden life" and the preparation of new methods which would serve a more effective prevention and elimination of its symptoms. These materials were subsequently published in April 1975 (Warsaw) under the title "Negatywne przejawy podkultury wieziennej: Srodki i sposoby przeciwdziałania" [Negative symptoms of prison subculture: Measures and methods of counteraction]. In this chapter I cite opinions voiced during discussions at the conference and contained in the materials published by the Central Administration of Penal Institutions.

8. Cf. J. Korecki, director of the penitentiary department of the Central Administration of Penal Institutions; S. Wrona, deputy director of the penitentiary department of the Central Administration of Penal Institutions; J. Gorski, psychologist, employee of the Central Administration of Penal Institutions, in "Negative Symptoms of Prison Subculture," pp. 12-38 (paper).

9. J. Korecki, S. Wrona, J. Gorski (Central Administration of Penal Institutions), "Negatywne przejawy," p. 16 (report).

10. W. Szeler, director of the penitentiary department of the detention center in Warsaw-Białołeka, in "Negatywne przejawy," p. 191.

11. B. Zajac, psychologist, senior counselor of the Voivodship Administration of Penal Institutions in Cracow, in "Negatywne przejawy," p. 124.

12. Plutowski, director of a correctional institution in Malbork, in discussion, in "Negatywne przejawy," pp. 112-17. The difficult situation in correctional institutions and hostels for juveniles is indicated by the use of the prison staff. Cf. *Dz. U. M.S.*, Warsaw, 20 June 1983, no. 3, n. 12, and ruling of the Minister of Justice of 1 June 1983 concerning the discontinuation of active service by functionaries of the prison staff in certain reformatories and hostels for juveniles. This pertained to the institutions in Malbork, Swiec, Cracow-Witkowice, and Białystok.

13. Zajac, in "Negatywne przejawy," p. 124.

14. P. Rymarski, director of the Voivodship Administration of Penal Institutions in Wrocław, in the discussion, in "Negatywne przejawy," p. 148.

15. K. Parciak, warden of the Detention Center in Warsaw-Białołeka, in the discussion, in "Negatywne przejawy," pp. 185-86.

16. J. Swieconek, director of the penitentiary department of the penal institution in Iława, a voice in the discussion, in "Negatywne przejawy," p. 192.

17. T. Szewczyk, deputy director of the security department in Strzelce Opolskie, a voice in the discussion, in "Negatywne przejawy," p. 160; ibid., other participants in the discussion.

18. J. Korecki, S. Wrona, and J. Gorski (Central Administration of Penal Institutions), paper in "Negatywne przejawy," as well as other voices in the discussion.

19. Ibid., pp. 27 and 32.

20. K. Strzepek, judge, head of department in the Department of Criminal Cases of the Ministry of Justice, in the discussion, in "Negatywne przejawy," p. 157.

21. Korecki, Wrona, and Gorski, in "Negatywne przejawy," p. 26.

22. Strzepek, in "Negatywne przejawy," p. 159.

23. W. Kupiec, judge of a Voivodship Court, the penitentiary department in Wrocław, in the discussion, in "Negatywne przejawy," p. 138.

24. K. Braun, psychologist in the penal institution in Tarnow, in the discussion, in "Negatywne przejawy," p. 145.

25. Moczydłowski and Rzeplinski, "Zatrudnienie wieziniow w polskim systemie penitencjarnym" [The employment of prisoners in the Polish penitentiary system] in *Praca skazanych odbywajacych kare pozbawienia wolnosci,* T. Bojarski et al., p. 25.

26. T. Judycki, director of the Voivodship Administration of Penal Institutions in Szczecin, in the discussion, in "Negatywne przejawy," p. 128.

27. Korecki, Wrona, and Gorski, in "Negatywne przejawy," p. 31.

28. Zajac, in "Negatywne przejawy," pp. 1224-25.

29. Plutowski, "Negatywne przejawy," pp. 118-19.

30. Szewczyk, "Negatywne przejawy," p. 160.

31. Rymarski, "Negatywne przejawy," p. 149.

32. "Wytyczne Dyrektora CZZK z dnia 2 kwietnia 1975 r. w sprawie przeciwdziałania i zwalczania negatywnych przejawow podkultury wieziennej" [Guidelines of the director of the Central Administration of Penal Institutions of 2 April 1975 on the counteracting and overcoming the negative symptoms of prison subculture] in *Przepisy w sprawie zakresu i organizacji pracy penitencjarnej w zakładach karnych i aresztach sledczych* [Regulations concerning the range and organization of penitentiary work in penal institutions and detention centers], CZZK MS [Ministry of Justice], Warsaw, June 1977, pp. 132-42.

33. Ibid., p. 133.

34. The informers describe everything, and in particular those symptoms of "hidden life" which were described in the "Wytyczne Dyrektora CZZK z dnia 2 kwietnia 1975 r."

35. Cf. Podgorecki, "Drugie zycie."

36. Cf. also, Goffman, *Asylums,* pp. 15-22.

37. Cf. M. Zalewska, P. Moczydłowski, P. Sawicka, "Pojecie 'ja' u przestepcow: Wstepne sprawozdanie z badan" [The concept of 'I' among the offenders: An introductory report on research] in *Wybrane zagadnienia problematyki przys-*

tosowania [Select problems of the problems of adaptation] (Warsaw: UW, 1979), pp. 85-100.

38. The data are taken from a Ph.D. thesis by T. Bulenda, entitled "Samouszkodzenia skazanych odbywajacych kare pozbawienia wolnosci w swietle przepisow prawa i ich stosowania" [Self-mutilation by convicts in confinement in light of legal regulations and their application], Department of Law, Warsaw University, 1982, p. 330. The sources of the data were reports of the penitentiary department of the Central Administration of Penal Institutions. Self-aggression in penal institutions and detention centers in Poland from 1965-1980: in 1965, 1,098; 1966, 1,147; 1976, 1,801; 1968, 2,690; 1969, 3,565; 1970, 4,867; 1971, 4,941; 1972, 2,635; 1973, 1,602; 1974, 1,212; 1975, 1,448; 1976, 1,435; 1977, 1,976; 1978, 1,876; 1979, 1,836; and 1980, 1,871.

39. Many of the phenomena examined in this section correspond with the postulates formulated during prisoners' protests in 1981. Their list is contained in Moczydłowski and Rzeplinski's "Warunki i problemy"; this is an incomplete list and the inmates demanded among other things the rights and duties resulting from the universally accepted regulations for the working prisoners (vacations, benefits, suitable work conditions, compensation, pensions); an increase payment received up to 50 percent, and for those paying alimony, up to 80 percent of the basic wage; the payment of 100 percent wages for 3 months prior to discharge, and this sum should not be subject to payment of court fees; equal wages for equal work for prisoners and civil workers; an improvement of the treatment of inmates who had committed self-inflicted injuries by: (a) an adequate number of beds in the cell for the number of prisoners; (b) shortening the period of waiting for an operation; (c) the recognition as sick bays those cells in which the inmates are isolated, only if they meet certain requirements; isolation of sick inmates from the other prisoners and the provision of suitable medical aid; an explanation of placing convicts and detainees who have financial obligations in cell blocks for the nonworking; reinstatement of preventative x-rays; raising the rates for food and improvement of the quality of the food; in the canteen, guaranteed amounts of tobacco products and food articles within limits foreseen by rations for all citizens, with the exception of articles whose consumption in prison is forbidden; granting white bread [preferable in Poland to dark bread]; guarantee of a meal to the inmates working outside for more than 8 hours; permission for working inmates to rest in bed during the day; granting of two additional hours of sleep on days free from work; guarantee of adequate quantity of personal hygiene articles and facilities; abandoning the practice of marking prisoners' clothes with the letters "ZK" [penal institution] and an improvement of the appearance of the clothes; permission to receive food and cigarettes during visiting hours; an exchange of aluminum dishes for enamel ones; issuing prisoners cutlery, razor blades, and shavers; guaranteed access to all types of mass media (the press, radio, and television) without treating them as forms of cultural or educational work; restoration of prison recreation halls converted for administrative and production purposes, and more access to these halls; permission to view films; permission for the prisoners to build a playing field for volleyball and basketball; subjection of the prison medical personnel to the supervision of the Ministry of Health and the employment of a suitable number of such

personnel; an increase of the influence of the penitentiary departments on the life of the inmates; an increased number of counselors and psychologists; relieving the counselors of administrative work; introduction of a prohibition of applying group responsibility; abolishing solitary confinement cell blocks; a verification of the principle of classifying prisoners as dangerous offenders; prohibition of the use of physical force by the prison staff and prohibition of truncheons, tear gas, and other measures; abolishing the penalty of the triple strap; abolishing the disciplinary punishment of depriving the inmates of cultural or educational activities; abolishing the censorship of correspondence in the lighter regime prisons; freedom of correspondence with state institutions and the abolition of censorship; a guarantee that cells are to be searched only in the presence of the senior member of the given cell, while body searches are to be performed only by a person of the same sex; the right to the receipt of a single food package of up to five kilos, once a month; the equalization of the norms of space for each inmate with international norms; the guarantee of a bed for each inmate; the provision of facilities for study in secondary prison schools; non-confinement of invalids and mentally ill inmates; the destruction of articles appropriated during a search in the presence of their owner; an improvement of conditions of transporting the prisoners; the bringing to justice of functionaries guilty of: (a) beating the prisoners, hanging the prisoners by their limbs on the barred windows, and using other forms of repression; (b) forcing the prisoners to make false statements by using various forms of pressure; (c) employing the prisoners on their own private estates and animal farms for building purposes; (d) wastefulness and the theft of the prisoners' property and state property; (e) assaulting passive convicts, participants of protests; (f) breaking the law in 1976; the dismissal from service of specific functionaries; the removal of specific functionaries from work with prisoners; an end to the employment in the same prison of related functionaries; the recalling of certain functionaries from their posts; a change of the attitude of certain foremen to the inmates in the place of work. Cf. also works of Moczydłowski and Rzeplinski, and Bojarski et al., *Praca skazanych odbywajacych kare.*

40. Also the regional authorities influence these decisions of the administration of the penal institutions; hence, the choice of the enterprises is limited.

41. One of the participants in the discussion, Judge K. Strzepek, the head of a department in the Department of Criminal Cases in the Ministry of Justice, thought that membership in the "code users" was a valid reason for denying discharge (since it might indicate an incomplete rehabilitation) and, therefore, that "code users" membership should be disclosed in motions for conditional release. "In the work of the Cracow court, membership in the 'code,' which was connected with negative attitudes of the convict, was accepted as the grounds for a negative prognosis of the future life of discharged inmates, and for this reason the court refused to grant conditional release. It appears to me that this sort of a practice cannot be questioned." See Rymarski, "Negatywne przejawy," p. 158.

42. The exploitation of the inmates for building private houses became so widespread that the Minister of Justice was compelled to issue a special order forbidding this practice. See *Dz. U. M. S.* document no. M-1195/76 of 29 April 1976 concerning the prohibition of using the convicts for the construction of private

houses and the use of transportation and machines (unpublished). These practices could be applied in those institutions where the inmates can serve sentences in a lighter regime and where employing them outside the prison bounds is permitted. On the rigors of confinement, see "Regulamin wykonania kary," op. cit.

43. Korecki, Wrona, and Gorski, in "Negatywne przejawy," pp. 18-20.
44. Swieconek, in "Negatywne przejawy," p. 193.
45. Korecki, Wrona, and Gorski, in "Negatywne przejawy," p. 15.
46. H. Machel, deputy director of the penal institution in Gdansk-Przerobka, in the discussion, in "Negatywne przejawy," p. 106.
47. S. Wrona, deputy head of the penitentiary department of the Central Administration of Penal Institutions, an introduction to papers, in "Negatywne przejawy," pp. 9-10.
48. K. Braun, in "Negatywne przejawy," pp. 144-45.
49. "I would like to say that a discussion, and preparation of more profound, precise analyses and prevention measures is necessary. These studies and works have to be closed, however, for at least a certain period of time, to a group of experts, people who are to some measure bound by propriety or who understand that one cannot perceive the phenomena of subculture as an interesting topic for the press or to use them for other similar purposes." See W. Taraszkiewicz, deputy prosecutor of the General Attorney's Office, in "Negatywne przejawy," p. 179.

8. Among the "Screws"

1. Not wishing to repeat myself, I omitted from this chapter information about relations within the community of the functionaries, which was discussed in chapters 2, 6, and 7.
2. In 1980 the prison staff "included about 17,000 functionaries (of which 4,000 were officers). . . . Within the particular departments (security, penitentiary, records and housing, financial, economic, and medical) the majority is composed of functionaries of the security department. In 1979 for every ten functionaries, six were employed in this department including 88 percent junior officers. The penitentiary departments were especially understaffed. The requirements here were for 2,000 persons (in October 1980, there were 1,242 employees, with about 10 percent working as psychologists)." See Moczydłowski and Rzeplinski, "Warunki i problemy," p. 469.
3. A. Mazurkiewicz, "Raport badawczy z pilotazu do badan empirycznych nad statusem społecznym i prawnym funkcjonariuszy SW" [A research report from an introduction to empiric investigations on the social and legal status of the functionaries of the prison staff], Warsaw, April 1980, mimeographed text. The dissatisfaction of the functionaries was revealed distinctly in 1981 during protests of the prison staff in various penal institutions, including those in Włodawa and Nowy Wisnicz. The appeal of the functionaries of the penal institution in Włodawa proclaims, "Our work is dirty, and we deal with the social scum. In a certain sense this is non-humanitarian work, since it is directed against people, even if they are evil, and there is no social acceptance of the profession of a 'screw' since, as a

result of excessive secrecy, the opinion about us is created by the inmates and their families who are automatically negatively inclined to the institution and its workers; actually, such an opinion should be produced by objective and thorough publications. People cannot tolerate more orders, and not in theory, but mostly in practice, with no compensation for the many additional duties during periods of intensified watchfulness, alert, alarms, and pursuit. Last year we had eighty days altogether of additional duty on Sundays and free Saturdays. It is not without reason that the majority of the young people maintain that they prefer 1000 złoty while at ease than 2000 for standing at attention." See Moczydłowski and Rzeplinski, "Protesty zbiorowe w zakładach karnych, raport z badan w problemie miedzyresortowym" [Group protests in penal institutions in Poland in 1981], MR.III/18 Warsaw: IPSiR, UW, 1982.

9. Social Relations in "Hidden Life"

1. Goffman, *Asylums*.
2. The essence of this variable is to express whether in a given enterprise technical possibilities exist for illegal production; it would be difficult to imagine this form of trafficking in an enterprise producing, for instance, fifteen-ton blocks of reinforced concrete.
3. Cf. F. H. Allport, "A Structuronomic Conception of Behavior: Individual and Collective," *Journal of Abnormal and Social Psychology,* vol. 64 (1962), pp. 3-30; see also K. E. Weick, *The Social Psychology of Organizing* (London: Addison Wesley, 1979).
4. Cf. Allport, "A Structuronomic Conception of Behavior."
5. Cf. Katz and Kahn, *Społeczna psychologia organizacji,* p. 39.

Index

PAWEŁ MOCZYDŁOWSKI is Director General in the Ministry of Justice, Director of the Central Prison Administration in Poland, and a sociologist at the Institute for Social Prevention and Resocialization at Warsaw University.